SO-ARL-592

THE COMING DESTRUCTION OF THE BAPTIST PEOPLE

A BRIEFING FOR PARENTS AND LEADERS

JAMES R. BELLER

 PRAIRIE FIRE PRESS

ST. LOUIS, MISSOURI

"WE SHALL DO WELL, BOTH AS CITIZENS AND AS CHRISTIANS, IF WE WILL HARK BACK TO THE CHIEF ACTORS AND LESSONS IN THE EARLY AND EPOCH-MAKING STRUGGLES OF THIS GREAT WESTERN DEMOCRACY, FOR THE FULL ESTABLISHMENT OF CIVIL AND RELIGIOUS LIBERTY—BACK TO THE DAYS OF WASHINGTON AND JEFFERSON AND MADISON, AND BACK TO THE DAYS OF OUR BAPTIST FATHERS, WHO HAVE PAID SUCH A GREAT PRICE, THROUGH THE LONG GENERATIONS, THAT LIBERTY, BOTH RELIGIOUS AND CIVIL, MIGHT HAVE FREE COURSE AND BE GLORIFIED EVERYWHERE."

—GEORGE W. TRUETT

© 2005 by James R. Beller
All rights reserved
Printed in the United States of America

ISBN 0-9668766-4-4

Prairie Fire Press
St. Louis, Missouri

Dewey Decimal Classification: 302
Subject Headings: Social Psychology Christian Life
                     Sociology---Foreign Opinion

All scripture quotations are from the King James Bible.
All emphasis in quoted material is the author's unless
otherwise specified.

For more information visit
baptistchristianworldview.com

Augustine, the progenitor of *the Old World Order*,
who laid the ax to the root, and severed ties
with the ancient church.

Contents

Introduction

The Baptists of America are in mortal danger. Our churches face extinction and our principles extermination. Our enemies deem our principles dangerous. The antichrist himself will not tolerate our theology and practice.

This book is about antichrist, and the *New World Order*. It is about the foundations of American government and the direction of our country. It is about Baptist principles and the foundation of liberty.

> "To destroy a people you must first sever their roots."
> —Alexander Solzenitisyn

The dismantling of the Baptist churches has been an ongoing thing, which we will prove in this book. And there are questions that demand answers.

Why is our Baptist Christian heritage hidden from us?

How did it happen? Is it not strange, even frightening?

How is it our children do not know their own heritage?

What are the issues? And what is at stake?

As we shall discover, the issues are the return of the Lord, and the principles of civil government. These issues are the greatest issues in life. Our view of the return of the Lord and our view of human government rule our lives.

What is at stake? The very existence of a denomination that breathes life into world Christianity. What is at stake is the foundation of American liberty, and with it the future of our country. That is probably difficult to believe, but it really isn't difficult to prove.

The Religious Right in America has amassed great wealth and political power in the past thirty years. Some of it has come at the expense of the Baptists. What Baptist people do not know is that some of our association with the right wing has damaged us. It has damaged our churches and especially our unique school system. And it has had a dulling effect on our home schools. But just as someone may freeze to death by falling asleep in the snow, the Baptists are numb to the dangers. It is of preeminent importance that we awaken.

> This book has been written for one reason: to awaken a sleeping group of people before their principles are totally destroyed.

This book has been written for one reason: to awaken a sleeping group of people before their principles are totally destroyed. Whether you believe it or not, this country is dependent upon Baptists maintaining their principles. As we shall discover, **"American principles are, basically Baptist principles."** Those principles are immortalized in the Declaration of Independence.

How Baptists are in danger of being destroyed can be illustrated by the words of Alexander Solzenitisyn: **"To destroy a people you must first sever their roots."** Solzenitisyn should know, he saw his own native Russia destroyed by deceit, propaganda, and revolution.

We shall examine the severing of three primary roots of the American Baptists: *Ancient Ancestry*, *Revival Heritage* and *American Principles*. We will discover how those roots have been cut off from the Baptists of today. In our discovery, we will come face to face with the actions of the **Catholic and Reformed,** who throughout history have waged a campaign of disregard, deceit, and death against the Baptists.

Specifically, our discovery will expose the actions of the modern "catholic Reformed *Reconstructionists*" in their quest to reconstruct the Baptist school and home school movements.

We Baptists are making some terrible mistakes. We have abdicated our pulpits and classrooms to our enemies without knowing the full background of the so-called culture war. While we have been sleeping, or dazed with the work of the ministry, our adversaries have been cutting away at our fundamental principles.

A recent survey of seven major preaching conferences was made examining the sermons delivered to a needy Baptist public. Sermon content was examined to see the thrust of the messages and especially to determine the illustrations used to make the teaching clear. A tally of quotes was also noted. The results are indicative of the direction and mindset of the Baptists. There was no reference to the ancient or American Baptists in the messages. None. No references to any of the great leaders of the Baptists in American history. The only Baptist mentioned was Charles Haddon Spurgeon. When coupled with the nearly non-existent references to the Baptists in our grade school and high school curriculum, this is alarming.

> I challenge you to ask your children to name a great Christian from the past. Preachers, ask your congregations. Other than Spurgeon, they couldn't name a Baptist. Ask them to name a great ball player and they will give you dozens. Our enemies have been very successful in their attacks.

Baptist Christians need to mend their ties to the Donatists, the Waldensians, the Paulicians, John Clarke, Roger Williams, Obadiah Holmes, Thomas Gould, Shubal Stearns, John Leland, Isaac Backus and the host of Baptist sufferers and patriots. Never heard of them? Why not? The Presbyterians know the names of John Calvin, John Knox, Jonathan Edwards, Gilbert Tennet, and John Witherspoon. The Methodists know the names of John and Charles Wesley, Sam Jones and Gipsy Smith. I guarantee Fundamentalists know the names of Dwight Moody, J. Wilber Chapman and Billy Sunday. None of these men, though they were great, were Baptist. These men did not suffer like our forefathers suffered, and believe it or not, neither were their works as great.

Is it not strange that Baptists don't know their greatest evangelists: Jeremiah Moore, Daniel Marshall, Abraham Marshall, John Taylor, Alfred Taylor, and the host of the Separate Baptists? Is it not strange that Baptists are not acquainted with the greatest church builder of the 18th and 19th centuries: Shubal Stearns? Or the greatest of American statesmen, Roger Williams, John Clarke and Isaac Backus? Or the greatest American missionary, Isaac McCoy? I challenge you to ask your children to name a great Christian from the past. Preachers, ask your congregations. Other than Spurgeon, they couldn't name a Baptist. Ask them to name a great ball player and they will give you dozens. Our enemies have been very successful in their attacks.

The Roman Catholic Church and her doctrines are easily identifiable and contrary to Baptist principles. However a subtler enemy to the Baptists is the catholic Reformed. Some might argue that the influence of the catholic Reformed upon Baptists is a Trojan horse, a stealth operation aimed at destruction from within. However, evidence will show that their influence is more *assimilation*, destruction by unification. Baptists are supposedly "Re-formed" from "Mother" church, and our only difference with Protestants is immersion. And since immersion has only existed since *1641, it is not important.

The end of such doctrine is powerlessness, loss of distinction, and the triumph of Antichrist. Our forefathers knew this. We don't.

---

* According to the theory of William H. Whitsitt.

Part 1: First Severance
Ancient Ancestry

Part 1: First Severance—Ancient Ancestry

Chapter 1
A Matter of Great Surprise

We now begin the first part of our briefing.
The first blow of the ax laid to Baptist roots was something called "Whitsittism."

"ALL who know much of the Baptist denomination must have regretted that so few are acquainted with its early history…it remains **a matter of great surprise that our own congregations should be, for the most part, uninstructed in the past doings of our body.**"
—Charles Spurgeon

Charles Haddon Spurgeon, perhaps the most respected Baptist of all time, expressed surprise[1] that Baptist people were uninstructed in their early history. It remains a surprise, as "our own congregations" remain "uninstructed." This is at once enigmatic and downright sinister. Spurgeon certainly wanted to remedy the "surprise." His inquiry into the situation centered on ancient Baptist history.

Until 1899, **every** Baptist historian in the world acknowledged the Baptists as ancient people tracing their principles back to Christ and His disciples. **Every** Bap-

---

[1] *The Sword and the Trowel*, August 1868.

tist historian held this view. If Spurgeon was surprised in his day that congregations were uninstructed, he would be shocked to know in our day, neither congregations nor pastors are instructed.

Here is a list of Baptist historians who believed Baptists to be ancient:

John Spittlehouse (1652)
Theilman J. Van Braught (1660)
Henry D'Anvers (1670)
Thomas Crosby (1740)
Isaac Backus (1770)
David Benedict (1813)
Joseph Ivimey (1830)
G. H. Orchard (1830)
J. M. Cramp (1868)
William Cathcart (1887)
Thomas Armitage (1888)
J. M. Carroll (1901)
John Taylor Christian (1926)

One would think that pedobaptist (infant baptism) historians from Roman Catholic, Congregational, Methodist, or Presbyterian backgrounds would try to discredit the ancient nature of the Baptists. Surprisingly, the best of the pedobaptist Protestant historians freely admitted that Baptists were ancient and could be found dissenting very early from the Catholic Church:

> The Mennonites [Anabaptists] consider themselves as the descendants of the Waldenses, ...The Mennonites are not entirely in error when they boast of their descent from the Waldenses, Petrobrussians and other ancient sects...Before the rise of Luther and Calvin, there lay concealed in almost all the countries of Europe, who adhered tenaciously to the following doctrine which the Waldensians, Wyclif-

fites and the Hussites had maintained...[2]—John Lawrence Mosheim (German Reformed historian.)

I should not readily admit that there was a Baptist church as far back as 100 A.D., although without doubt there were Baptist churches then, as all Christians were then Baptists.[3]—John Clark Ridpath (Methodist historian.)

For that matter, the most esteemed Roman Catholic historians believed that Baptists were ancient, and that their principles could be traced to the time of Christ. In 1565, Stanislaus Hosius, Roman Catholic theologian and president of the Council of Trent wrote:

> There shall be no faythe more certayne and true, then is the Anabaptistes, seeyng there be none nowe, or have bene before time fore ye space of these thousand and two hundred years, who have bene more cruelly punyshed, or that have more stoutely, stedfastly, cherefully take theire punishment, yea or have offered them selves of theire owne accorde to deathe, were it never so terrible or grevouse. Yea in Saint Augustyn his time, as he hymselffe sayth, there was a certaine monstrouse desire of deathe in them.[4]

After 1899, those that held to the belief that Baptists were ancient were labeled as "Landmarkers," or "Trail of Blood adherents," or "Baptist Briders." This is strange, seeing the long line of classic Baptist historians could not possibly be labeled in this manner.

We will remain undaunted and in the spirit of Spurgeon, our desire is to go back and repair the severed roots to our ***ancient*** Baptist forefathers.

---

[2] John Lawrence Mosheim, "History of the Mennonites or Anabaptists," *Ecclesiastic History* (New York: Harper Bros., vol. 2, 1871), 128.

[3] W. A. Jarrell, *Baptist Church Perpetuity or History* (Dallas, TX: By the Author, 1894), 59.

[4] Stanislaus Hosius, Byshop of Wormes in Prussia, *A Most Excellent Treatise of the Begynnyng of Heresyes* (Antwerp: Aeg Diest. 1565, reprint, Yorkshire, England: The Scholar Press Ltd., 1970), 44.

In order to do that, we will need to have some background on *the way the world was*, under **the *Old World Order*.**

Our heritage is rarely, if ever, referenced in our pulpits and classrooms. Baptist people simply are in the dark concerning their own testimony. This should be cause for alarm, for in our ignorance we are rendering ourselves powerless against the devil and antichrist:

> Rev. 12:11 And they overcame him by the blood of the Lamb, and **by the word of their testimony**; and they loved not their lives unto the death.

Chapter Two
The Old World Order

With so much talk about the *New World Order*, it may be interesting to know that the *New World Order* is pushing an agenda very much like the *Old World Order*.

In truth, we may define the *Old World Order* as **the way the world was before there was an America**.

What was the world like under the *Old World Order*?

To answer this question thoroughly would take hundreds of pages, but for our purposes, since this is a *briefing*, we will be brief.

History pivots on the life of Christ. After his death, burial and resurrection, his followers, called "Christians," preached the Gospel to the known world. Their accomplishments were astounding, so much so that Pagan Rome perceived them to be a threat to their government.

The Roman civil government chose to persecute the Christians, killing them wholesale, burning them, feeding them to wild animals, and blaming them for all the ills of society. There were 14 major persecutions lasting until the year 312 when the era of Pagan Roman was superceded by the era of "Christian" Rome.

For the first three hundred years of Christian history, the believers were scattered in their local assemblies, administered by pastors (bishops). They had fellowship with one another because of common doctrine. There was no hierarchy, no central control, no dominion over the state, no church-state relationship at all.

Most Christians were looking for Christ to return, to right the tragic wrongs, and take His proper place as ruler of the nations. Nearly universal was the belief that Jesus had fulfilled the Old Testament covenant and that the churches were a part of a new covenant or New Testament.

Keeping with the catch phrases of the present generation, we may say that the ancient world had a "Pagan Worldview."

The ancient church also had a worldview. We may properly call it the "Pauline Worldview." As you can tell, the Pauline Worldview, based on the religion of Jesus Christ, stood in opposition to the Pagan Worldview (still very much in existence).

In the time of the primitive or ancient church, these worldviews were in conflict. However, the military aspect of the conflict was carried on by just one side, the Pagan side. Christians did not use weapons, nor did they establish military organizations. Christians did not submit to the state-church marriage of paganism.

> **The Pagan Worldview**
> 1. Gods exist to give power.
> 2. Gods must be appeased for favor.
> 3. You may choose (or create) your own god according to your desires.
> 4. The state (world), and the gods are one in power. The God of choice would rule in a theocracy.
> 5. The Pagan theocracy was a counterfeit of the old Hebrew theocracy.
> 5. Corporeal or capital punishment is justified for "heretics" who reject the State-god.

Around the year 313 an incredible change took place. Emperor Constantine changed the religion of Rome from Paganism to "Christianity." He professed Christianity and not only tolerated the Christians, he made their religion the new established religion of the empire. Without going into too much detail, Christians, by way of an emerging "catholic" church would now have dominion over society the way the ancient Hebrews had dominion in their theocracy. But not every church wanted to be a part of the hierarchy.

The first group to resist the emerging church hierarchy was the Novatianists. Of the Novatianists Charles Spurgeon wrote:

> Novatian held that apostasy was a sin which disqualified them from again entering into church fellowship, and to secure a pure community, he formed a separate church, which elected him for its pastor. These purer churches multiplied, and continued in existence for more than three centuries, the members being everywhere looked upon as Puritans and Dissenters. They were Anabaptists, baptising again all who had been immersed by the orthodox and corrupt church. **The Novatians, then, were Baptists.**[5]

The Pauline Worldview
1. Jesus fulfilled the Old Testament Covenant. The New Testament begins a new covenant.
2. The New Covenant is individual, not patriarchal.
3. Baptism is immersion for believers only.
4. Regeneration is a work of the Holy Ghost, occurring at salvation.
5. There is a coming future reign of Christ (1,000 years) (Chilasm)
6. Christ's return is imminent.
7. The church is not Israel, and is separate from the world (state). As such, the local church is "a garden enclosed."
8. The New Testament churches do not punish "heretics."
9. The churches are comprised of "pilgrims" or strangers in this world awaiting Jesus to return for them.

In fact, many groups of independent churches arose from 313 to 1640. You may view their areas of ministry on the map on the next page.

---

[5] Charles Spurgeon, ***The Sword and the Trowel***, August 1868.

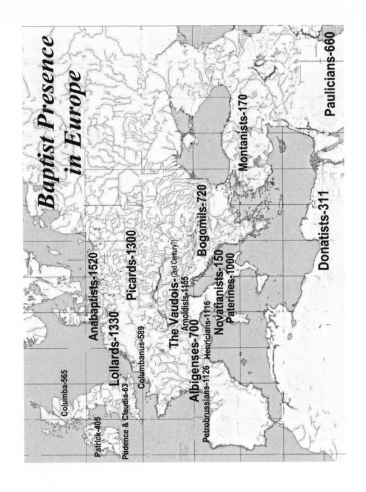

Who were these people? And why did they separate from the Catholic Church?

Following the Novatianists, next to resist catholic control were the Donatists of Carthage, North Africa. They simply wanted to choose their own pastors without the presbytery of the establishment hindering them. The Donatists insisted they were independent, and declared their religious liberty. One would think that would have been the end of it. But here would the memory of the Hebrew theocracy be brought before the emerging Catholic Church. The Hebrew Theocracy, ordained by God, had been scattered by His judgement. Now the Catholic Church would regain that theocracy.

As we have stated, not all Christians believed in the new theocracy. There simply was no scripture command for the church to assume theocratic religious and civil rule. The Donatists were a group of churches that rejected the theocracy and hierarchy of the Catholic Church.

R. J. Rushdoony, considered to be the "father of American home schooling" observed, "Donatism, held that there could be no validity in any act by any church which did not separate itself from the world in Donatist terms. After the fifth century, **Donatism as a church ceased to be a consequential problem.**"[6]

Rushdoony's quote begs the question, "What happened to the Donatists?" Fortunately, David Benedict, the famed Baptist historian of the early nineteenth century supplies an answer:

...the Emperor at the same time issued an edict whereby he called upon the North African Christians to return back to the unity of the church. Of the failure of this convert scheme for gaining the Donatists, forcible measures were the next resort. The Donatists now were to be deprived of their churches, and they were actually fallen upon by armed troops while assembled in them for the worship of God.

[6] R. J. Rushdoony, *Christianity and the State*, (Vallecito: Ross House Books, 1986), 105.

Hence followed the effusion of blood, [starting in 347] and the martyrdoms of which the Donatists so often complained of their adversaries.[7]

This was the first enforcement of the Catholic Church Theocracy on record. The theocracy would grow in power.

It came to pass that a bright, articulate, and charismatic young scholar and philosopher named Augustine rose to prominence in the African church. He became the Bishop of Hippo. One of his most important tasks was to rid the Catholic Church of the Donatist schism.

A prolific writer, Augustine determined that the Donatists needed to be brought back into Mother church. As schismatics, the Donatists had denied the true faith by standing apart from the Holy Catholic and Apostolic Church. Augustine, reinforcing the new theocratic government of the Church, called for the execution of all Donatists who would not recant and turn back to their Mother. And thus began the *dark ages*.

How the *Old World Order* Came into Power

Augustine believed the Catholic Church was the new Israel and as such had jurisdiction over the religious affairs of civil society. This jurisdiction meant armed enforcement. Never mind that the covenant of the Old Testament was uniquely made to Israel and Israel alone. Augustine made his opinions "orthodoxy," quite frankly because he had the military clout to do so.

---

[7] David Benedict, *History of the Donatists* (Pawtucket: Nickerson, Sibley and Co., 1875), 32.

In reality, Augustine created a false "Christian World-view."

Augustines' orthodoxy disavowed the new covenant by merging the new covenant with the old. He made infant baptism the door to *the Church* and the sign and seal of the covenant. The church was to be "universal," or "catholic." There would be only one church and its power would control "all of life." After several hundred years of this kind of thinking, the marriage of church and state was established. All those denying the church-state establishment and its initial door of entrance, infant baptism, were to be punished.

Augustine wrote, "We think it is as lawful for us to ask assistance against [the Donatists], as it was for Paul to employ a military force against the conspiration of factious men." To which David Benedict answered, "This is a new version of the conduct of the Apostle Paul."[8]

> **The Augustinian Worldview:**
> 1. Mankind inherits Original Sin.
> 2. Baptism is a symbol and sign of the covenant (figurative of circumcism) and washes away Original Sin.
> 3. Infant "baptism" is compulsory and provides regeneration.
> 4. The church is Israel (figurative interpretation of scripture).
> 5. Membership in the Universal Church not voluntary.
> 6. Sacerdotal salvation through *the Church*.
> 7. Predestination and Election before being born or born again.
> 8. The New Covenant is patriarchal, not individual.
> 9. The events of Revelation are figurative and Jesus return is not imminent (Amillennialism)
> 10. Corporeal or Capital Punishment upon heretics.
> 11. Church-State marriage, the world dominated by *the Church*.

Augustine employed the services of the military commander, Macarius in his war on the "heretic" Dona-

---

[8] Ibid.

tists. The Donatists began referring to the Catholics as "Macarians."

Benedict observed, "Optatus (an enemy of the Donatists) argued that the killing of the Donatists by Macarius in his war against them for heresy, **was sanctioned by Moses killing three thousand for worshiping the golden calf, and Phinehas and Elijah for those they killed.**"[9] This is standard thinking for the Augustinians, who believe the church to be Israel.

The Catholic Church, with a theological engine designed by Augustine, viewed itself as the theocratic equal of Israel in the Old Testament times. Infant baptism was the sign and seal of the New Covenant; the New Covenant was a continuation of the Old Covenant; and the New Covenant had a new administration, THE CHURCH.

So, through the centuries, those dissenters (Baptist Christians, for the most part) were systematically condemned as heretics for rejecting infant baptism and refusing the control of the Catholic Church.

The punishment of heretics stained history for 1,000 years. The most heinous heresy: re-baptism.[10] The list of the persecuted baptized believers includes (but is certainly not limited to) these groups:

Donatists (398)

Paulicians (690)

Petrobrussians (1126)

Albigensians (Bogomils) (1238)

Vaudois (Waldensians) (Possibly as early as the second century,[11] officially condemned in 1487.)

---

[9] Ibid., 38.

[10] The Baptists did not believe their baptism to be "ana" or "re" baptism. Baptism without a profession of faith (conversion) was NO baptism.

[11] J. T. Christian, quoting Rainerio Sacchoni, "...some say that it [the Waldensian schism] dates back to the time of Sylvester (325), others to the time of the apostles." *History of the Baptists, Vol. 1* (Texarkanna, TX: Bogard Press, 1922), 72. Both Samuel Moreland and Peter Allix affirm the existence of the Vaudois before the time of Peter Waldo.

Anabaptists (1530)
Lollards (1575)

Were any of these groups heretical? Certainly there were some doctrinal deviations. But as the classic Baptist historians have recorded on numerous occasions, their similarities to the Baptists of today are striking. Their most outstanding characteristic was immersion for believers only (rejecting infant baptism).

They suffered for that striking similarity. For instance, according to Augustus Neander, the Lutheran historian, the number of martyrs among the Paulicians alone was not less than 100,000.[12] This was the *Old World Order*.

The Reformation

Centuries passed. The Roman Catholic institution drifted from some of Augustine's theology and embraced Thomas Aquinas in various circles. She sank into rituals and placed a "Pope" at her head. It was obvious she needed reforming.

Martin Luther came first. In 1517, Luther published his 95 theses against the Catholic Church and marked the beginning of the *Protestant* movement.

In 1529 at the Diet of Speyer, the term *Protestant* was used to describe the Reformed. No Baptists were recognized as a part of that group.

Of the 95 complaints Luther held against Romanism, none was in opposition to the Roman Catholic church-state. Luther was very much in favor of using the sword to enforce the authority of the Augustinian church-state. Jews, and especially "heretics" were a target of the Augustinian Luther. Luther wrote:

> ...they [the Anabaptists] are not only blasphemous but also seditious men, **let the sword exercise its**

---

[12] Augustus Neander, *General History of the Christian Religion* (London: Bell and Daldy, 1869), vol. VI, 340.

rights over them. For it is the will of God, that he shall have judgment who resisteth the power.[13]

Then, John Calvin began his reforms. Calvin is credited with resurrecting Augustine. Calvin wrote and ruled from Geneva from 1541-1564.

Just as Luther had done, John Calvin did not break from the Catholic Church. He attempted to "re-form" her.

How the *Old World Order* Stayed in Power

John Calvin restated the Augustinian "Christian Worldview," He wrote:

Augustine frequently made of this passage against the Donatists, to prove that godly princes may lawfully issue edicts, for compelling obstinate and rebellious persons to worship the true God, and to maintain the unity of the faith; for, though faith is voluntary, yet we see that such methods are useful for subduing the obstinacy of those who will not yield until they are compelled.[14]

If Calvin's worldview looks familiar, it is because it is simply Augustinianism with two slight changes. First:, while

Calvin's Worldview:

1. Mankind inherits Original Sin.
2. Baptism is a symbol and sign of the covenant (figurative of circumcision) and washes away Original Sin.
3. Infant "baptism" is compulsory and provides regeneration.
4. The church is Israel (figurative interpretation of scripture).
5. Membership in the catholic Reformed Church not voluntary.
6. Sacraments are a "means" to grace through *the Church*.
7. Predestination and Election before being born or born again.
8. The New Covenant is patriarchal, not individual.
9. The events of Revelation are figurative, Jesus will return at the conclusion of a 1,000 reign of the catholic Reformed Church. (postmillennialism)
10. Corporeal or Capital Punishment upon heretics.
11. Church-State marriage.

---

[13] Arthur B. Strickland, *Roger Williams* (Boston: The Judson Press, 1919), 72.

[14] See Calvin's *Institutes*, Commentary on Matthew, Mark, Luke, volume 3.

Augustine was full blown sacerdotal with his plan of salvation, Calvin viewed the sacraments to be a "means" to grace. The problem is Calvin's followers never have known what he meant by "means." Consequently, the Presbyterians and the Reformed easily apostatize into baptismal regeneration. Second: Rather than "Amillennial" (not believing in a millennial reign of Christ), Calvin is "Postmillennial," opening a door to "Dominion." This negates the imminence of Christ's return.

Any way you look at it, Calvinism sustained Augustinianism. As Loraine Boettner, respected Reformed theologian wrote, "**The Reformation was essentially a revival of Augustinianism.**"[15]

The catholic Reformed *Old World Order* sustained the theocracies of Europe and England and continued to doom the Baptists. Phillip Schaff wrote:

> The Reformers refused to others the right of protest which they claimed and exercised for themselves, and the civil magistracy visited the poor

Anabaptists with capital punishment.[16]

The picture (left) is a statue of Huldrich Zwingli, the Reformer of Zurich. It shows him in his role as church-state enforcer. He holds his Bible in one hand and a sword in the other. This is evidence of the church-state marriage continued by the Reformers (Lutheran and Calvinist).

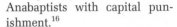

[15] Loraine Boettner, *The Reformed Doctrine of Predestination* (Phillipsburg, PA: Presbyterian and Reformed Publishing Co., 1932), 370.

[16] Pillip Schaff, *History of the Christian Church* (Grand Rapids, MI: William B. Eerdmans Publishing Co., 1910, reprinted 1977), vol. VIII, 67.

Calvinism spread to Scotland under the preaching of John Knox, where the *Old World Order* became known as Presbyterianism.

In England, the *Old World Order* was sustained as Anglicanism.

These catholic Reformed branches of Protestantism held to the baptism, civil government, eschatology and basic church government of their Roman "Mother Church." Those who differed were burned, drowned or killed with the sword.

Yet, as their enemies destroyed them, the ancient Baptists survived and even multiplied. And they began to petition to end the persecution. With the age of printing dawning, at long last their pleadings with princes and kings began to be published and read.

One typical Baptist plea was the words of Leonard Busher petitioning the King of England in 1614:

> ...I humbly desire his majesty and parliament, with all godly carefulness, to consider that it is not possible that the church of Rome, called catholic, or those that are descended of her, and have received their ministry and ordination from her, ever was, or could be, the apostolic church, called primitive church; or she that is descended from her.

(Scene on left is of the Baptist Edward Wightman, burned in Litchfield, England, 1611.)

> Suffer not your bishops to destroy those men and women that strive to serve God, according to his word. Be not your bishops' executioners in burning, banishing, hanging, and imprisoning of harmless and peaceable Christians; but let them enjoy freedom of the gospel and liberty of conscience: so that the apostolic church, which is scattered and driven into the wilderness and desert

16

of this world, may be again gathered together, both Jews and Gentiles, into visible and established congregations. And that the catholic and universal church of antichrist may be consumed and abolished, by his Spirit, as the holy apostle hath foretold.—Leonard Busher, 1614.

In Colonial America, **it is clear the Puritans**[17] **lived according to the** *Old World Order.* From the establishment of the Massachusetts Bay Colony in 1630, they denied citizenship to Baptists and banished dissenters who refused to keep silence.

The Puritans of New England hung those they deemed witches, and with the noose broke the necks of

the poor Quakers. They banished Roger Williams, John Clarke and the opinionists.[18] They beat William Witter, executed fair Mary Dyer and whipped Obadiah Holmes. The Reformed Church of England with Presbyterian

---

[17] We should be careful to differentiate the *Pilgrims*, who were Separatists and much more mild, from the *Puritans*, who enforced their theocracy with a vengeance.

[18] See the author's book, *America in Crimson Red.*

troops drove the Separate Baptists out of North Carolina.[19] This was the *Old World Order*.

The scene above (courtesy of the Baptist History Preservation Society) depicts the beating of Obadiah Holmes. The "consistent" Christians of the Puritan "covenant way" were the perpetrators. This happened in Boston, Massachusetts in 1651. Holmes crime: he assisted in conducting an unauthorized Baptist church service. Only by the grace of God did he survive the beating. **Look at the picture**. The picture depicts a catholic Reformed officer of the court holding Holmes sentence. One will never find in the pages of history a Baptist holding such an order.

Europe and England were under the *Old World Order* theocracy of the Church. Infant baptism was the sign of citizenship and the door of entrance to the Church. The rise of the American republic would change that. Chapter seven of our briefing will detail that amazing story.

Let us state once more: **our heritage is rarely, if ever, referenced in our pulpits and classrooms**. Baptist people are in the dark concerning their own testimony.

Rev. 12:11 And they overcame him by the blood of the Lamb, and **by the word of their testimony**; and they loved not their lives unto the death.

The spirit of antichrist, the real author of the *Old World Order*, knowing this dynamic, has made every effort to hide or change the testimony of our ancient fathers. He has done this by discrediting the classic Baptist historians of the seventeenth, eighteenth, and nineteenth centuries. The twentieth century Baptist historians have rejected the findings of their classic forefathers. We will now reveal the source of their rejection as we examine the ax blow laid against our ancient roots by one William H. Whitsitt.

---

[19] George Washington Paschal, *History of the North Carolina Baptists* (Raleigh: Edwards and Broughton Co., 1930, 1955).

Chapter Three
Antichristian Forgery

> The official reports of the proceedings against the Anabaptists are from their enemies, and are more or less colored. The works of Anabaptists are few and scarce.—Phillip Schaff[20]

From the time of the Donatists to the rise of the Anabaptists in Zurich, Baptist people and their writings were consigned to the flames. Up until the time of the printing press, Baptist enemies could simply lie about the "anabaptists" and their claims would be unchallenged. But with the onslaught of printing, our apologists began writing. And they were opposed. The opposition usually applied the bald-faced lie as their weapon. Sad to say, the catholic Reformed were the biggest perpetrators. Dr. Philip Schaff, Presbyterian Professor in Union Theological Seminary, and the most prominent church historian of his time wrote:

> In 1674, Richard Baxter claimed that Baptists were generally immoral. Baxter would have been happy if the Baptists were put to death. Henry D'Anvers, one of the earliest of English Baptist historians referred to his claims as "antichristian forgery."

> The history of the Anabaptists of the Reformation period has yet to be written from an impartial, unsectarian standpoint. **The polemical attitude of the Reformers against them has warped the judgment of historians**. They were cruelly treated in their lifetime by Romanists and Protestants, and misrepresented after their death as a set of heretical and

---

[20] *The Baptist Quarterly Review*, New York, 1890, vol. 12, No. 43.

revolutionary fanatics who could not be tolerated in a Christian state.[21]

One of the first of the catholic Reformed to bear false witness against the Baptists was Richard Baxter. In 1674, Baxter claimed that Baptists were generally immoral. Baxter would have been happy if the Baptists were put to death. Henry D'Anvers, one of the earliest English Baptist historians referred to his claims as "antichristian forgery."[22]

In 1730, after being stonewalled by the Reformed historian Daniel Neal, English Baptist historian Thomas Crosby struck out on his own to write the classic, *History of the English Baptists*. Neal had a large number of Baptist archives, records and testimonies, which he chose to suppress. Much of what Neal possessed was never recovered.

In 1780, John Leland, famed Baptist pastor and evangelist of Virginia and New England, complained of the writings of the catholic Reformed Presbyterian Henry Pattillo:

> A late author, Rev. Mr. [Henry] Pattilloe, in giving an account of the rise of other societies, says, "the Baptist made their appearance in Germany, soon after the Reformation began." Has the good Mr. Pattilloe got this by wrote, hearing of it so often? or has the judicious pen of Mr. Smith [John B. Smith, President of Hampden-Sydney College] helped him out in a dead lift? ... let the Rev. gentleman remember, that **the Baptists can produce sacred proof for their appearance in Judea, about fifteen hundred years before those tumults in Germany.**[23]

---

[21] Ibid.

[22] Henry D'Anvers, *A Treatise of Baptism* (London: By the Author, 1674, reprint Harrisonburg: Sprinkle Publications, 2004), xxiv.

[23] John Leland, *The Writings of Elder John Leland* (New York: G.W. Wood, 1845), 121.

These few examples show the rancor of the enemies of the Baptists. But the time came when Baptist historians turned the gun on themselves. The enemies of the Baptists no longer needed to accuse and distort the records of our forefathers. Our own historians did it for them. The gun of historical suicide was purchased and loaded by Dr. William H. Whitsitt.

Whitsitt was the son of James Whitsitt, a great pioneer preacher in Tennessee. He attended Juliet Academy and studied for the ministry under James Madison Pendleton at Union University in Jackson Tennessee. He graduated in 1861, and served as a Civil War chaplain for the Confederate Army. After the Civil War, he continued his studies at Southern Baptist Seminary, receiving an advanced degree in 1869.

In a move that proved disastrous, Whitsitt chose to continue his studies at the University of Leipzig and the University of Berlin. This was at the height of German *rationalism*, which polluted the seminaries of Germany.

Returning to America in 1871, he pastored for a while in Georgia, and became a professor at Southern Baptist Seminary in

William H. Whitsitt

Louisville, Kentucky. He eventually became the president of the seminary.

Seemingly unrelated, in 1880, a series of anonymous articles began to appear in the Congregational newspaper, the *New York Independent*. The articles challenged the Baptists on immersion. The articles claimed that immersion was lost as the Gospel mode of baptism and not reinstated by the English Baptists until 1641. On September 9, 1880, an article reported:

It was not until the year 1644, three years after the invention of immersion, that any Baptist confession prescribed "dipping or plunging the body in water as the way and manner of dispensing the ordinance.[24]

No one knew who wrote such inaccurate ideas about ancient Baptist history. The articles from the *Independent* were largely forgotten.

In the spring of 1896, William Whitsitt wrote an article about the Baptists for *Johnson's Encyclopedia*. The article stated his theory that the English Baptists did not begin to baptize by immersion until 1641, when a portion of the "Anabaptists" began immersing.

> It was clear that Whitsitt undermined the principles of the Baptists while being employed by the sacrifices of Baptist people.

The "Theory of 1641" set off a firestorm of opposition. Henry M. King of Rhode Island; Dr. J. H. Spencer, the Kentucky Baptist historian; and Dr. T. T. Eaton, editor of the *Western Recorder* immediately responded to Whitsitt. It was revealed that Dr. Whitsitt, was the author of the infamous but now almost forgotten set of articles, which appeared in the *New York Independent* in 1880.

John Taylor Christian,[25] a Baptist pastor in Mississippi, began to study the files of the *Independent* and found other editorials in which the Baptists were attacked. It was clear that Whitsitt undermined the principles of the Baptists while being employed by the sacrifices of Baptist people.

Whitsitt wrote, "...if in the future it shall ever be made to appear that I have erred in my conclusions, I would promptly and cheerfully say so."[26]

---

[24] William Dudley Nowlin, *Kentucky Baptist History, 1770 -- 1922* (Louisville: Baptist Book Concern, 1922), 142-154.

[25] J. T. Christian later authored *A History of the Baptists*, released in 1926.

[26] William Dudley Nowlin, *Kentucky Baptist History, 1770 -- 1922* (Louisville: Baptist Book Concern, 1922), 142-154.

David Benedict had already proven Mr. Whitsitt to be inaccurate. William Cathcart, in his definitive *Baptist Encyclopedia*, included several articles which proved Whitsitt to be in error. The brilliant Thomas Armitage devoted much of his *Baptist History* of 1890 to prove that immersion was practiced throughout continental Europe

> *Whitsittism* insisted that Baptists did *not* exist until the Reformation. It was the tool the *adversary* used to reconstruct the Southern Baptists of America into Protestants. Since the independents share a mutual history with the Southern Baptists, it has also affected them. **It was the blow that severed ties with the ancient Baptists.**

and England in all ages. G. H. Orchard, in direct response to Whitsitt, wrote a compelling history of the Baptists. Most vigorously, John Taylor Christian, who made numerous trips to Europe in research, proved beyond question the errors of Whitsitt. Publication after publication showed him to be in error. B. H. Carroll, S. H. Ford and W. W. Everts opposed the "1641 Theory." The response to his desire to be shown in error was truly overwhelming.

In Ford's *Christian Repository*, for January of 1897, Dr. Joseph Angus, famed English Baptist preacher and writer cited the existence of 26 Baptist churches practicing immersion **before** 1641. Perhaps most telling, he gave the names of at least 21 pamphlets opposing the "dippers" (Baptists) and their manner of IMMERSION, all written *before* 1641.

Mr. Whitsitt never did admit his error and was dismissed from Southern Baptist Seminary in 1898.

However his "antichristian forgery" became accepted after his death. His "English Descent Theory" became the official stance of the Southern Baptist Convention. In 1905, a large number of Baptists disagreed with the Whitsitt stance, withdrew from the convention, and formed the American Baptist Association.[27] (Landmark Baptists)

Historians A. H. Newman, W. W. Barnes, W. J. McGlothlin. and Henry Vedder, followed Whitsitt in the next generation. Vedder, a modernist historian from Crozer Theological Seminary in Pennsylvania, released his *Short History of the Baptists* in 1907. Vedder[28] was refuted by J. T. Christian, but still became the most widely read Baptist historian of the early twentieth century. Vedder was widely used among Independent Baptists.

> What denominational label would you place on someone who believed in salvation by grace, who baptized by immersion upon a profession of faith, who believed the Bible to be without error and believed in a regenerate church membership?

Whitsittism insisted that Baptists did *not* exist until the Reformation. It was the tool the *adversary* used to reconstruct the Southern Baptists of America into Protestants. Since the Independent Baptists share a mutual history with the Southern Baptists, it has affected them also. **It was the blow that severed ties with the ancient Baptists**.

During the twentieth century, Baptist historians Robert Baker, Leon McBeth, Walter Shurden, Robert G. Torbet, James Edward McGoldrick, etc., and Fundamentalist historian, David Beal, all marched lockstep with a man who was proven wrong in his own generation. The modern Baptist historians simply argue that *Whitsittism* is "scientific."

---

[27] This group, the ABA, is not to be confused with the Northern Baptist Convention, which became the American Baptist Convention. (ABC)

[28] G. W. Paschal wrote of Vedder, "About the same time, Professor H. C. Vedder of Crozer Seminary published a paper in which it was argued that the Baptist position on baptism was untenable." *Paschal Papers* (Winston-Salem: Z. Smith Reynolds Library), PCMS 86 4/382 p. 12.

However, I agree with John Leland when he declared our Baptist heritage "extends to the Jordan River." This declaration can be proven scientifically.

We should believe the Bible to be scientifically correct when it declares:

> **Ephesians 3:20-21** Now unto him that is able to do exceeding abundantly above all that we ask or think, according to the power that worketh in us,
> Unto **him** be glory **in the church** by Christ Jesus **throughout all ages,** world without end. Amen.

> **Matthew 16:18** And I say also unto thee, That thou art Peter, and **upon this rock I will build my church;** and **the gates of hell shall not prevail against it.**

> **Matthew 23:34** ¶ Wherefore, behold, **I send unto you prophets, and wise men, and scribes**: and some of them ye shall kill and crucify; and some of them shall ye scourge in your synagogues, and persecute them from city to city:

There are three obvious promises from the above scriptures.

1. Jesus was to receive glory IN THE CHURCH THROUGHOUT THE AGES.
2. The "gates of hell" WOULD NOT PREVAIL AGAINST the church.
3. Jesus promised to send to the church PROPHETS, WISE MEN AND SCRIBES— and they were to SUFFER.

Scientifically, through research and deduction, could you find the prophets, wise men and scribes? If Jesus promised the church would stand, suffer and glorify Him THROUGHOUT THE AGES would you be able to find the church?

I ask our Whitsittite scholars a very simple question: **What denominational label would you place on someone who believed in salvation by grace, who baptized by immersion upon a profession of faith, who believed the Bible to be without error and believed in a regenerate church membership?** The honest answer is: Baptist. The hypothetical question describes the primitive church in the book of Acts. It follows scientifically that Baptists are ancient and are not a part of the Reformation.

Spittlehouse, Van Braught, D'Anvers, Crosby, Backus, Benedict, Ivimey, Orchard, Cramp, Cathcart, Armitage, Carroll, and Christian all claimed that Baptists were ancient. And every great Baptist leader including William Williams, Octavias Winslow and Charles Spurgeon believed it. Why did they claim this? Because the evidence proved their existence.

Suppose a wanted poster surfaced for John Dillinger circa 1932. According to our modern Whitsittite historians, the poster would be meaningless. They would insist that scientifically, Dillinger probably did not exist. The Whitsittite scholars might argue that the wanted poster is not scientific enough. To the rest of us, it wouldn't matter, it would be obvious that the Whitsittites must be **ignoring the obvious**, and perhaps not even worthy a hearing.

We know the Baptists are ancient because of the wanted posters. Here are a few:

- The council held at Carthage in 398, under Aurelius, against those who denied original sin, infant baptism, and predestination.
- A.D. *413*, Against The So-Called Anabaptists, by the two Eastern Emperors, Theodosius And Honorius: "If any minister of the Christian church is found guilty of having rebaptized any one, he, together with the person thus rebaptized, provided

the latter is proved to be of such an age as to understand the crime, shall be put to death."[29]

- A.D. 421, anabaptism condemned by edict of Constantius
- In 535 an Imperial edict condemned the Donatists
- 1139—Arnold of Brescia condemned by the Lateran Council for rejecting infant baptism
- 1176—Alexander III condemns the Waldensians for errors and impieties (anabaptism)
- In 1183, the Albigensians were condemned by Pope Lucius
- 1229—the infamous Council of Toulouse condemned both Albigensians and Waldensians
- On November 19, 1526, the Council of Zurich declared that anabaptism should be punished by drowning. Zwingli concurs.
- In 1535, an edict was issued by Emperor Charles V against the Anabaptists.

Zwingli scientifically identified the Anabaptists as "Baptists" at the Council of St. Gall, on September 9, 1527. An edict under his direction declared:

In order that the dangerous, wicked, turbulent and seditious sect of the **Baptists** may be eradicated, we have thus decreed:

If any one is suspected of **rebaptism**, he is to be warned by the magistracy to leave the territory under penalty of the designated punishment. Foreign **Baptists** are to be driven out; if they return they shall be drowned.[30]

---

[29] Henry D'Anvers, *A Treatise of Baptism* (London: By the Author, 1674, reprint Harrisonburg: Sprinkle Publications, 2004), 112.

[30] John Taylor Christian, *A History of the Baptists, Vol. 1* (Texarkanna, TX: Bogard Press, 1922), 121.

If these "heretics" were condemned for rejecting the baptism of the *Old World Order*, then as Spurgeon rightly judged, they were Baptists.

Which means that Whitsitt, Henry Veddar, Robert Baker, Leon McBeth, Walter Shurden, Robert G. Torbet, James Edward McGoldrick, et.al. have purposely or inadvertently perpetuated "antichristian forgery."

Could there be an orchestrated attempt to deliberately bear false witness against the testimony of the baptized believers?

That deserves some attention by way of an interlude in the next chapter.

END OF PART 1

Part 2: Second Severance Revival Heritage

Chapter 4
The Liars Interlude

We now begin the second part of our briefing.

The second blow laid to Baptist roots was the elevation of *Fundamental* heritage. We will discover how that happened, but first we will look at an important issue that will help us understand the rest of our briefing.

The complaints of *antichristian forgery* by Henry D'Anvers serve as a warning to us today. The enemies of the Baptists and Baptist Christian principles have not gone away. They are very much at work today, using the same tactics.

Forgery is the deliberate attempt to falsify a true record. Lies and deceit accomplish this. There is no other way to do it. Forgery has been perpetrated on the Baptists for centuries. The religion of Antichrist is false Christianity, and at times it looks so good.

Infant baptism might look good as a ceremony, but it is a counterfeit.

Postmillennialism might seem good to bring about change in society, but it is a counterfeit system.

The Reformed view of predestination might be a way to explain history, but it is a counterfeit way of viewing the timetable of God's dealings with man.

With the Catholic Church, sometimes the truth is hard to discern. Since the time of Augustine, the Catholic Church propaganda machine has done a number on the public. From false witness against the Donatists, to the ridiculous claims for the relics in the middle ages, the Catholic Church has maintained some fabulous lies.

What is harder to accept is the principles of the Reformed and lying. In particular, I am referring to the concepts made public by a group of theologians known as the catholic Reformed "Reconstructionists." Emerging in the late twentieth century, these radical Reformers have made public some scary strategy in their "war" for theocracy in America.

When the Reformed were marching in Europe and Scotland, in the sixteenth and seventeenth centuries, they were very much *crusaders*, using a literal sword to fight real battles for religious supremacy. They were literally slashing, clubbing, stabbing, piercing, trampling, strangling, burning, etc., to establish the Reformed faith (German Reformed, Lutheran, or Presbyterian). That is what theocracy does. While Baptists would do their best to defend their families, they could not march with Catholic or Reformed troops to establish a baptism in which they did not believe.

Many theologians and writers of the catholic Reformed are very much in favor of "warring" for religious establishment. In particular, the catholic Reformed *Reconstructionists* believe we are in the midst of war— right now. And they have a strategy. Everyone ought to be aware of their strategy.

The undisputed leader of *Reconstructionism* is the late Rousas John Rushdoony. Rushdoony was a disciple of Princeton Presbyterian theologian Cornelius Van Til. It was Rushdoony and his writings that are credited with the rise of the catholic Reformed Presbyterian *Reconstruction* movement of the 60's and 70's. Additionally, his writings are said to be responsible for the rise of the home school movement in America. His theology and philosophy have had an effect on the Baptists. Rushdoony died in 2001, but his philosophies continue to influence a large number of people.

Here is a classic Rushdoony passage, important to our briefing:

> But does God require us to **tell the truth at all times**? Such a proposition is highly questionable.[31]

---

[31] Rousas J. Rushdoony, *The Institutes of Biblical Law, A Chalcedon Study with Three Appendices by Gary North*

Rushdoony then spends twenty pages justifying lies in the case of deceiving an enemy. He further states:

> This truth-telling means, not the exposure of our privacy, but bearing a true witness in relation to our neighbor. It does not apply to acts of war.[32]

One wonders if Rushdoony is aware of SILENCE. The concept of SILENCE in the face of an enemy, such as is practiced by the U.S. military (name, rank, and serial number) is of course, the best policy. Jesus practiced silence before Pilate. Silence is a right of the accused in any court in America, and is the best way to keep information from an enemy.

Mr. Rushdoony is at least plain on where he stands concerning the establishment of religion in America. It is not a Baptist stand:

> *Reconstructionism* is "a version of the Reformed, Postmillennial Theology that emphasizes the concepts of Theonomy and Dominion."

> ...no disestablishment of religion as such is possible in any society. ...**there can be no tolerance** in a **law-system** for another religion.[33]

Rousas John Rushdoony is a catholic Reformed Presbyterian theologian who believes in religious establishments in civil government (the *Old World Order*). He also apparently believes it is acceptable to **lie** in times of war. In short, he could rightly be termed an Augustinian. This may explain his failure to tell us the fate of the Donatists back in chapter two.

What is *Reconstructionism* exactly? Andrew Sandlin, former president of the Chalcedon Foundation,

---

(Phillipsburg, PA: Presbyterian and Reformed Publishing Co., 1972), 543.

[32] Ibid., 544.

[33] Ibid., 5.

the original *Reconstructionist* organization, said Christian *Reconstructionism* is "a version of the Reformed, Postmillennial Theology that emphasizes the concepts of Theonomy and Dominion."

By definition, the *Reconstructionists* are classic Augustinians. And they are for the most part Calvinist Presbyterians.

In the beginning of their movement, the *Reconstructionists* were willing to discuss their strategy. This is not so today. Today every *Reconstructionist* will flatly deny any association with the movement. But in the early 1980's the *Reconstructionists*, under R. J. Rushdoony and his son-in-law, Gary North, formed the Geneva Divinity School, headquartered in Tyler, Texas.

The school published three books in a series called *Christianity and Civilization*. The books contain their theology and plan for the reconstruction of the American Republic. Those books are:

- *The Failure of the American Baptist Culture*, 1982.
- *The Theology of Christian Resistance*, 1983.
- *The Tactics of Christian Resistance*, 1983.

Contained in these books is the strategy of lying. Here is one of their theologians, Jim West:

> The Christian has no obligation to speak truthfully to those who have forfeited the right to hear the truth. The commandment **does not say that "thou shalt never tell a lie."**[34]

> First, the term situation ethics, is, per se, one that we do not find to be repugnant for the simple reason that there is a situation for all ethics.[35]

> The commandment does not say that thou shalt never lie.[36]

---

[34] Jim West, "Rahab's Justifiable Lie," *Christianity and Civilization 2: The Theology of Christian Resistance* (Tyler, TX: Geneva Divinity School, 1983), 73.

[35] Ibid., 72.

[36] Ibid., 69.

Even the famous Reformed lawyer, John White-head, founder of the Rutherford Institute, apparently approves of the lie strategy:

Rahab risked everything in order to follow the laws of God, **including telling lies.**[37]

While you attempt to fully digest the above statements, it is disconcerting to note that R. J. Rushdoony, though he approves of the "lie strategy," has complained about "false witness" in history books. The nature of his complaints is inconsistent with his own philosophy. Rushdoony complained in his *Institutes of Biblical Law*:

The false witness born during World War II with respect to Germany is especially notable and revealing. The charge is repeatedly made that six million innocent Jews were slain by the Nazis, and the figure—and even larger figures—is now entrenched in the **history books.**[38]

I am not saying Mr. Rushdoony was a Nazi sympathizer, but for whatever reason, some of his followers certainly are. You may want to your own research. Do an internet search on "Rushdoony" and "white supremacy." Try googling "Rushdoony" and "neo confederate," or "Rushdoony" and "nazi,"and you will get the picture.

The catholic Reformed Presbyterian *Reconstructionists* also love to be associated with the Scottish Covenanter military. Again, you may want to your own research.

---

[37] John Whitehead, "Christian Resistance in the Face of State Interference" *Christianity and Civilization 3: The Theology of Christian Resistance* (Tyler: TX, Geneva Divinity School, 1983), 8.

[38] Rousas J. Rushdoony, *The Institutes of Biblical Law, A Chalcedon Study with Three Appendices by Gary North* (Phillipsburg, PA: Presbyterian and Reformed Publishing Co., 1972), 586.

Reconstructionist apparent disdain of Baptist principles and theology is of the same nature that was harbored by the Catholic Church toward the Novatianists, Donatists, Paulicians etc. And it is understandable, for the *Reconstructionists* have freely admitted they are Augustinians.

Chapter 5
Comatose from an Accident

We now return to the task at hand.

The second blow laid to Baptist roots was the elevation of *Fundamental* heritage over *Baptist* heritage. I believe it was an accidental blow, and was never meant to sever us from our testimony, but it happened.

Bible-believing Baptists of the twenty-first century have a *dual* heritage. We are *Fundamental* and *Baptist*. One heritage has been forsaken. Allow me to lay some groundwork.

In May of 1999, I attended a Baptist history tour of New England. Somewhere in Rhode Island in a wooded abandoned cemetery, I stood at the foot of the grave of Obadiah Holmes. I wept as I heard the story of his suffering for the cause of liberty in America. Holmes, the Baptist preacher, was beaten nearly to death for holding an "unauthorized" church service in Massachusetts. His blood ran like a river from Boston Townhouse square, the same square visited with the blood of the patriots at the Boston Massacre.

I cannot number the times I had heard, "Sadly there were NO great Baptist evangelists," or, "the great camp meetings were the invention of the Presbyterians," or, "the greatest revivals were a product of Finney, Moody, Sam Jones and Billy Sunday."

Baptists have the greatest legacy of evangelists America has ever produced: Jeremiah Moore, Stearns, Daniel Marshall, Abraham Marshall, Samuel Harriss, John Waller, John Taylor, and Jeremiah Vardeman, to name a few.

I do not remember when I had wept so violently. My tears were shed for two distinct reasons. First, I was overwhelmed by the sacrifice of this Baptist preacher for the sake of my liberty, and second, I could not **believe** that I had **never heard of him**.

I was ashamed of myself and I hurt for his testimony. And I determined that at least in my own ministry, Obadiah Holmes and others like him, would not be forgotten.

I just assumed that Baptists had always operated on the edge of acceptance. Since I had never heard a word from the pulpit about Baptist heritage I assumed we must have been sort of backward. I cannot number the times I had heard, "Sadly there were NO great Baptist evangelists," or, "the great campmeetings were the invention of the Presbyterians," or, "the greatest revivals were a product of Finney, Moody, Sam Jones and Billy Sunday."

I often thought, "at least the Baptists had Charles Spurgeon." "Perhaps Adoniram Judson made up for our ineptness." "Wasn't Talmage a Baptist? No?!"

> The disturbing truth is that **our heritage is rarely, if ever, referenced in our pulpits and classrooms**. The Baptist people of 2005 may have never heard of Holmes, Clarke, Williams and Backus, but secular historians of the nineteenth century certainly had.

I was doomed to believe all of that until I ran headlong into the testimony of the early Baptists of America. My heart was set on fire as I heard the testimony of John Clarke and Isaac Backus. I was thrilled at the power of God in the life of Shubal Stearns and the Separate Baptist revival of the South.

Think for a minute. If it was illegal to be a Baptist in this country until just before the Revolutionary War, how did the Baptists become the largest non Catholic group of Christians in America? The answer is Shubal Stearns and the Separate Baptist revival.

Baptists have the greatest legacy of evangelists America has ever produced: Jeremiah Moore, Stearns, Daniel Marshall, Abraham Marshall, Samuel Harriss,

John Waller, John Taylor, and Jeremiah Vardeman, to name a few.

The Baptist people of 2005 may have never heard of Holmes, Clarke, Williams and Backus, but secular historians of the nineteenth century certainly had. Here the oft-quoted nineteenth century historian George Bancroft comments on the beating of Obadiah Holmes:

> When Clarke, the pure and tolerant Baptist of Rhode Island...began to preach to a small audience in Lynn, he was seized by the civil officers...He and his companions were tried, and condemned to pay a fine of twenty or thirty pounds; and Holmes, who refused to pay his fine, was whipped unmercifully.[39]

Professor J. L. Diman on the Baptists and the forming of Rhode Island wrote:

> Thus for the first time in history a form of government was adopted which drew a clear and unmistakable line between the temporal and the spiritual power, and a community came into being which was an anomaly among the nations.[40]

The famous Judge Joseph Story, whom David Barton is so fond of quoting, said this about Clarke and Williams and the government of Rhode Island:

> In the code of laws established by them, we read for the first time since Christianity ascended the throne of the Caesars, the declaration that conscience should be free and men should not be punished for worshiping God in the way they were persuaded He requires.[41]

As a matter of record, a surprising number of Americans, (not necessarily Baptists) were at least acquainted with the *principles* of the Baptists and their

---

[39] George Bancroft, *History of the United States, Vol 1* (Boston: Little, Brown, and Co., 1854), 450.

[40] Arthur B. Strickland, *Roger Williams* (Boston: The Judson Press, 1919), 28.

[41] Ibid.

love for liberty. Vernon Louis Parrington, who is considered in some circles as America's greatest literary historian, wrote this about Williams and the founding of Rhode Island:

> But when he went into the broad ways of Carolinian England, seeking the rose of Sharon and the lily of the valley, he discovered only abominations...And so as a Christian mystic Roger Williams became a Separatist, and set his mind upon the new world where the lover might dwell with his bride.[42]

We shall examine the Baptist influence on liberty later in this briefing.

As we have stated, Bible-believing Baptists of the twenty-first century have *dual* heritage. We are *Fundamental* and *Baptist*. We have a *Fundamental* heritage that reaches back approximately 100 years to the time of the city-wide revivals under the famous evangelists of the nineteenth and early twentieth century.

We also have a heritage that reaches further back, to the ancient Baptists of Europe. And to the American heritage of liberty, to the frontier and the wilderness where a forgotten group of Separate Baptist evangelists gave birth to the greatest republic the world has ever known. **This is our *Baptist* heritage**.

Wake Forest University professor, G. W. Paschal wrote, "I make bold to say that these Separate Baptists have proved to be the most remarkable body of Christians America has known."[43]

The Separate Baptists were led by the incomparable Shubal Stearns, a converted New England Congregationalist, who after his baptism in Connecticut, migrated to North Carolina to fulfil the call of God upon his life.

---

[42] Vernon Louis Parrington, *Main Currents in American Thought*,
http://xroads.virginia.edu/~Hyper/Parrington/vol3/bio.html

[43] George Washington Paschal, *History of North Carolina Baptists vol. 1* (Raleigh: Edwards & Broughton Co., 1930), 240.

Stearns began preaching with a congregation of 17 in central west North Carolina and revival broke out. He soon had 17 preachers whom he trained and sent into Virginia and South Carolina. Within one generation over 1,000 churches were birthed and within two generations over 5,000 churches were birthed. In all actuality, the revival is still not over. The Southern Baptists; the Independent Baptists; the church of God, Cleveland, TN; and the Landmark Baptists, are direct descendants from Stearns and the Separate Baptists.

Our Separate Baptist forefathers broke the iron fist of tyranny prior to and after the War for Independence. Every American should have knowledge of the 44 preachers jailed in Virginia and the profound impact their **testimonies** had on Washington, Jefferson and especially Madison.

A number of these men were at one time household names among Americans. The following servants should be household names among our **Baptist** people:

Roger Williams
John Clarke
Obadiah Holmes
Isaac Backus
Elizabeth Backus
Samuel Stennett
Jeremiah Moore
Rachel Thurber Scammon

Shubal Stearns
Daniel and Martha Marshall
Abraham Marshall
William and Sara Murphy
Samuel Harriss
John Gano
John Leland
Adoniram Judson
John Taylor
Isaac McCoy
Jeremiah Vardeman
Hudson Taylor

It is as though we are in a coma; a coma caused by an unfortunate accident. What was the accident that caused the coma?

It appears to this author, that our *Fundamental* heritage overtook our *Baptist* heritage. Here is the accident report:

Prior to the Civil War, an attempt was made by the Pedobaptists (infant baptizers) to unify the non-Roman Catholic denominations in America. In the early days this effort was led by Henry Ward Beecher, the Boston Congregationalist. Beecher (right) believed that a "great evangelical assimilation" was coming to the United States.[44] It was known as "Christian Union." The Baptists largely rejected this idea fearing they would violate their principles.

In 1866, Baptist pastor and historian Thomas Armitage, publicly argued against the Baptists joining the Christian Union. Armitage explained that Baptists and Pedobaptists were diametrically opposed on the issue of baptism, and therefore were in disagreement about church membership, and what constituted a

---

[44] James R. Beller, *America in Crimson Red* (Arnold, MO: Prairie Fire Press, 2004), 473.

41

church. If Baptists were to hold communion (the Lord's Supper) with the Pedobaptists, then both the Baptists and the Pedobaptists would violate their own principles.

Just a few months after the courageous stand of Armitage, a new movement called the "Evangelical Alliance" began to take root. This movement was identical in essence with Christian Union. It greatly benefited the Congregational evangelists E. P. Hammond and D. L. Moody. Once again, the Baptists for the most part respectfully declined joining the Alliance. The Evangelical Alliance was a powerhouse. But problems arose.

From 1866, the colleges of all denominations were infiltrated and corrupted by German Rationalism. The age of **Modernism** began.

It was **Modernism** that prompted the birth of the **Fundamentalist movement**. **Fundamentalism** was an attempt to rescue the Evangelical Alliance from unbelief. The Fundamentalists tried to keep the Alliance pure from unbelief. The only way to do that was to begin their own institutions. This also caused the rise of Fundamentalist journals such as *The Fundamentalist* and *The Sword of the Lord*.

Thus were born schools such as Moody Bible Institute, Bob Jones College, Wheaton College, and Dallas Theological Seminary. None of these new schools were Baptist. They were formed with the Evangelical Alliance in mind. Their TESTIMONY was E. P. Hammond, D. L. Moody, Sam Jones, J. Wilber Chapman, Billy Sunday and Bob Jones. When Bible believing Baptist pastors sent their young preachers to be trained, they sent them to non-denominational schools which had the **Evangelical Alliance** as their testimony and heritage.

The Fundamentalist journals also took up the cause and pointed young Baptist preachers to the Evangelical Alliance. From 1900 to 1950, Baptist leaders were ingrained with the testimony and heritage of the Protestant Revivalists of the **Evangelical Alliance**. This effectively overshadowed both ancient Baptist heritage and American Baptist heritage. The old Baptists were forgotten. In my opinion, this was not done in malice or with intent to deceive. However, with the denominational Baptists already polluted with "Whitsittism," and the independent Fundamentalists rendered comatose, Baptist higher education was blinded to its own testimony on nearly every hand.

> Historically, Fundamentalists adhere to the five fundamentals outlined by the 1910 General Assembly of the Northern Presbyterian Church. These five fundamentals are:
> 1. Inerrancy
> 2. Virgin Birth of Christ
> 3. Salvation by Grace
> 4. Bodily Resurrection
> 5. The Second Coming of Christ.
>
> We hasten to say: Baptist principles of **believer's immersion, liberty of conscience, and the imminent return of Christ** are *fundamental* to our faith.

In the years 1950-2000, exclusive Baptist Colleges were founded but the problem of testimony and heritage was not corrected. Only in the last 5-7 years has there been an effort to teach Baptist history and heritage among Fundamental Baptists. Yet, we are still criminally ignorant of the testimony and heritage of our Baptist forefathers. Non-denominational schools, along with the new Baptist colleges inadvertently declared that Baptists are *Fundamental* first and *Baptist* second.

International Baptist Network
Illustrates this Critical Issue

Historically, Fundamentalists adhere to the five fundamentals outlined by the 1910 General Assembly of the Northern Presbyterian Church. These five fundamentals are: **1.** Inerrancy of the Scriptures **2.** Virgin

Birth of Christ **3**. Salvation by Grace by the Substitutional Atonement **4** Bodily Resurrection of Christ and **5**. The Second Coming of Christ.

Certainly, these are not evil principles, but their usage has resulted in weakening Baptist heritage *and* theology. We hasten to say: Baptist principles of **believer's immersion, liberty of conscience, and the imminent return of Christ are** *fundamental* **to our faith**.

To illustrate, I bring to your attention the 2005 formation of the **International Baptist Network**. Here are some excerpts from a report concerning its beginning:

> On February 9, 2005 at the Adolphus Hotel in downtown Dallas , the first public meeting of the International Baptist Network (IBN) drew representatives from more than three dozen denominations, theological seminaries, colleges and mission boards, and individual churches.
>
> ...a handful of Baptist leaders began looking at the New Hampshire Confession of 1833 as a foundational accord for their cooperation. That early group reformatted the articles, updated the language and **clarified the expressions of eschatology**, then christened it "The Georgia Baptist Confession."
>
> [In the meeting it was] stated, "**Our denominational labels are not doctrine**, and this meeting is not about denominational labels; this meeting is about **the fundamentals of the faith**."
>
> ...many of the Independent Baptists present in Dallas had at one time criticized the Southern Baptists for its "liberalism"... in 1979 the fundamentalists of the SBC began moving the Convention toward the right, the new leadership dealt with their liberal fringe elements...At the same time, many Independent Baptist groups have struggled with uncompromising members of the right over issues of second-degree separation, hyper-legalism and a King James-only Bible.
>
> [It was stated]...The IBN is possible because the SBC has dealt with its liberal left and Independent Baptists have dealt with its radical right."

What will hold together the International Baptist Network is **fundamental doctrine**. And what doctrine is fundamental to Christianity? **First**, the Bible is the inerrant, inspired Word of God without error, and is the only authority for Christians and churches. **Second**, Jesus was born of a virgin and is the God-Man. **Third**, the sinless Son of God died a substitutionary death for sinners and those who believe in Him can be forgiven of their sins and guaranteed a home in eternity with God. **Fourth**, the physical resurrection of Jesus Christ from the dead gives new life to all believers. **Fifth**, the bodily return of Jesus Christ at the end of this age will complete God's plan and purpose on this earth.[45]

So, to be clear, the new **IBN** is a *Fundamentalist* organization, based on the five fundamentals of the **1910 General Assembly of the Northern Presbyterian Church.** This means clouding of Baptist TESTIMONY. The **IBN** claims the Baptist New Hampshire Confession, but emphasizes the **Presbyterian** Five Fundamentals. This illustrates how Baptists continue to be severed from their roots.

---

[45] http://www.nljonline.com/
index.php?option=com_content&task=view&id=20&Itemid=2

Chapter 6
Postmillennial Interlude: Israel *Isn't*

> Rushdoony identified the underlying problem a generation ago: "Judaism grew out of the rejection of Jesus Christ and steadily became humanism, and the Talmud is essentially the exposition of humanism under the facade of scripture."[46]—Gary North

As we close out part 2 of our briefing, we need to consider a pivotal point of difference between the catholic Reformed Worldview and the Baptist Christian Worldview.

In catholic Reformed (Calvinist or Lutheran) doctrine, *the Church* is the new Israel, which means, to them, the real Israel is not Israel. In the *Old World Order* the Jews suffered under this system, as did every other independent religious body.

Today it seems that Israel *isn't*. This is poor foreign policy, based on poor theology. I believe the theology of the state department has changed.

Since 1948, the nation of Israel has had a friend in the United States. Our country has given financial and military support for the Jewish State since the day of its modern inception. Not only have we supplied Israel with aid, weaponry, and intelligence, we have supplied her with

> Jesus Christ will return as their Messiah prince and establish His kingdom, beginning a 1,000-year reign. This view was held by most ancient churches and was known as chiliasm (from the greek *chiliasmos* meaning, thousand). Today this theology is known as *premillinialism*. No surprise that Augustine condemned *chiliasm*.

---

[46] Gary North, *The Judeo-Christian Tradition* (Tyler, TX: Institute for Christian Economics, 1990), 152.

a large percentage of her population. One could safely say we have *loved* Israel.

The love for Israel was based on the American mind. The Jews were given their first refuge to practice their religion in Rhode Island. John Clarke saw to that. Religious liberty swept America and a re-examination of the primitive Christian view of last things became a part of the American mind: Israel is still God's nation, and God isn't finished with them. Moreover Jesus Christ will return, as their  Messiah prince and establish His kingdom, beginning a 1,000-year reign. This view was held by most ancient churches and was known as chiliasm (from the greek *chiliasmos* meaning, thousand). Today this theology is known as *premillinialism*. No surprise that Augustine condemned *chiliasm*.

But to the candid observer, love towards Israel seems to have grown cold during the current administration. Our president has instigated a "roadmap to peace," pressuring for unprecedented concessions to the enemies of Israel. What has happened? I believe the theology of the state department has changed.

The primitive Christians made a clear division between the Old and the New Testaments of the Bible. They also recognized a clear distinction in the manner in which God deals with mankind in each.

The word "testament" is another word for "covenant." The very idea of a *New* Testament insists on a *New* Covenant, not the continuation of the old.

Beginning with Augustine, the Roman and Protestant catholics used a *figurative* interpretation of the Bible. The church-state alliance is the *figurative* manifestation of ancient Israel's covenanted collective theocracy. Which of course means God is finished with Israel. Augustinians believe that the rule of the catholic

Reformed church will dominate the world and Christ will return after the church-state 1,000 year reign. This is a *figurative* view of the scriptures. Saying goodbye to Israel is a view of Reformed theology. This view is called *postmillennialism.*

The Baptists, picking up on their primitive ancestors, insisted on a *literal* interpretation of the Bible, instead. So it is to the New Testament, that they turned for their essential doctrines of the New Testament church. Christ's sacrificial death and resurrection had fulfilled Old Testament Law, and mankind is now living in the dispensation of *"grace."* In the Old Testament, God judged men individually, but He also judged them *collectively* as families and as nations and in particular, Israel. In the New Testament, God judges men  as *individuals*, and *only* as individuals. That has always been the view of ancient Baptist theology.

The Old Testament covenant with Israel was not intended as a model for the New Testament church. Nor was Israel's old covenant to serve as a pattern for the government of any nation except Israel.

Theology is the engine that runs life. And eschatology (study of last things) determines your view of civil government. Everyone has a theology, or a view of God. Everyone has a view of how God deals with man and man's final destiny.

There is a theology that teaches Israel as a special nation, *does not exist.* There is a growing theological worldview, rooted in Augustinianism that teaches that the modern state of Israel is not Israel, but a just a group of ethnic Zionists. That theology is catholic Reformed theology. Specifically, it is postmillennialism.

Consider this:

If amillennialism or postmillennialism is true, then:

- The Bible is not literally true
- Jesus return is NOT imminent.
- The events of Revelation took place sometime between the first and fourth centuries (preterism).
- The Beast (antichrist) is not a person, God is finished with Israel and the present state of Israel is simply a "Zionist" state.
- The Church *is* Israel and has the right to rule in a theocracy.
- If you are working toward a one-world theocracy, then you are inadvertently working for antichrist.

I believe the theology of our state department has changed. How do we explain the shift in support for Israel any other way?

END OF PART 2

Part 3: Third Severance
American Principles

Chapter 7
A Brief History of True Liberty

We now begin the third part of our briefing.

The third ax blow laid to Baptist roots is our Christian School system. For you to see this very important and sobering fact, you will need to get a handle on the true history of liberty.

George W. Truett, (left) famed pastor of the First Baptist Church of Dallas, Texas said,
"Ideas rule the world. A denomination is moulded by its ruling principles, just as a nation is thus moulded and just as individual life is thus moulded. Our **fundamental essential principles have made our Baptist people**, of all ages and countries, **to be the unyielding protagonists of religious liberty**, not only for themselves, but for everybody else as well."

The Baptists of America broke the tyranny of Europe and with it, the tyranny of Rome's *Old World Order.* Think not? Consider the words of George Bancroft:

The plebeian sect of the Anabaptists, "the scum of the Reformation," **with greater consistency than Luther** applied the doctrine of the Reformation to the social relations of life and threatened an end to kingcraft spiritual dominion, tithes and vassalage. They were trodden under foot with foul reproaches and most arrogant scorn; and its history is written in the blood of myriads of the German peasantry; but **its**

principles, safe in their immortality, escaped to Providence.[47]

The great Baptist leaders of the past certainly understood that Baptist principles and American principles were identical.

Dr. J. Q. Adams,[48] theologian and Baptist pastor of the Baptist church of Caldwell, New Jersey wrote:

> To the advocacy and propagation of the principles here presented, our country owes all it possesses of true greatness. **American principles are, essentially, Baptist principles**, and this is owing to the fact that Baptist principles have impressed themselves upon the nation, as the only principles consistent with a government... recognizing the universal right to civil and religious liberty.[49]

If the founding principles of America are found in the Declaration of Independence, then what are those principles and from whence did they originate? David Little, Harvard professor tells us:

> **John Locke's letters** on religious toleration and the freedom of conscience explicitly influenced the thought of **James Madison** and **Thomas Jefferson**, two founders who played such an important role in working out early legislative formulations of freedom. And Locke's ideas, in turn, are, with one or two exceptions, simply **restatements of the central arguments in favor of freedom of conscience developed by Roger Williams** in the middle of the seventeenth century, when Locke's opinions on these subjects were being shaped.[50]

---

[47] George Bancroft, History of the United States, Vol. 2 (Boston: Little, Brown & Co., 1879), 457.

[48] Adams book, *Baptists, the Only Thorough Religious Reformers* was considered by Spurgeon as the best manual of Baptist principles available. He used it in his Pastor's College.

[49] J. Q. Adams, *Baptists, the Only Thorough Religious Reformers* (reprint: Kessing Publishing, 2004), introduction.

[50] David Little, *Conscience, Theology, and the First Amendment* Cambridge: Soundings, Summer/Fall, 1989, 357-78.

We appreciate Little's thoughts, and we will prove the line and legacy of liberty in just a moment. As a reminder, here are the immortal words of Jefferson in the founding document of America:

> WE hold **these Truths** to be **self-evident**, that **all men are created equal**, that they are endowed by their **Creator** with certain **unalienable Rights**, that among these are **Life, Liberty and the pursuit of Happiness**—That to secure these Rights, Governments are instituted among Men, **deriving their just Powers from the Consent of the Governed,** That whenever any Form of Government becomes destructive of these Ends, it is **the Right of the People to alter or to abolish it**, and to institute new Government, **laying its Foundation on such Principles** and organizing its Powers **in such Form**, as to them shall seem most likely to effect their Safety and Happiness.

The basic principles outlined above by Thomas Jefferson serve as the *"foundation"* for our *"form"* of government. The form was then defined by the Constitution.

Throughout history, the signers of America's founding document, the Declaration of Independence, were correctly referred to as *the founders*, while those who signed the Constitution were known as *the framers* of the country. James Madison, the man most responsible for its design is often referred to as *the architect* of the Constitution. Some would call Madison *the father* of the Constitution.

There should be no doubt that the United States Constitution rests upon the founding principles of the Declaration of Independence.

For instance:

John Adams argued from the principles of the Declaration in the Amistad case before the Supreme Court.

John Hancock wrote that "this Declaration of Independence" is "considered as the ground and foundation of a future Government."[51]

President John Quincy Adams in his inaugural address of 1825, said the Constitution was "founded upon the republican principles of equal rights." Which of course is expressed in the Declaration.

In spite of this common knowledge, a leading figure in the Religious Right, William Einwechter wrote, "**to make the Declaration of Independence into a fundamental statement of the political philosophy upon which the United States was founded is both misguided and futile.**"[52]

Einwechter, in the same article quotes perhaps the mightiest pen of the *Reconstructionists*, Gary North, "A third myth is that the Declaration has, or once had, some sort of legal standing in American law. **It never had the force of law**. It was a very superior piece of wartime propaganda, but **it was no more legally binding than one of Thomas Paine's pamphlets.**"[53]

Why would anyone, claiming to be a part of the Religious Right, want to denigrate the Declaration of Independence? Could it be that the document is TOO Baptist? It pleads the cause of civil and religious liberty. And that was a Baptist dissenter issue.

The old Appleton's American Encyclopedia states the obvious:

> In England, from the time of Henry VIII to William III, a full century and a half, **the Baptists struggled to gain their footing and to secure liberty of conscience for all.** From 1611 they issued appeal after appeal, addressed to the King, the Parliament, and the people, in behalf of "soul liberty," written with a

---

[51] http://www.indiana.edu/~liblilly/history/hancocktext.html

[52] William Einwechter, "Declaration of Independence and National Renewal" (Pittsburgh, PA: *The Christian Statesman*, July-Aug. 2ooo)

[53] Gary North, *The Journal of Christian Reconstruction Vol 3 N. 1.* (Tyler, TX: Summer 1976), 104.

breadth of view and force of argument hardly since exceeded.[54]

Not a handful of Baptist Christians know this. I believe it would be difficult to find two dozen preachers who know much of anything about the influence of the Baptists on American government. Why?

The answer to that question should become obvious in just a little while, but let us turn our attention back to our *National Treasure*, the Declaration of Independence.

Much has been made over the years as to the origin and meaning of the principles of the Declaration of Independence. It was one of the two most important works of Thomas Jefferson. The other of great importance, according to Jefferson himself, was the *Virginia Statute of Religious Liberty*.

There is a report that Jefferson, "turned neither to book nor pamphlet" when he wrote the Declaration of Independence. Richard Henry Lee was convinced Jefferson copied the entire Declaration from John Locke, and John Adams said that it did not include a single original idea of Jefferson's.

Joseph Martin Dawson, writing for the *Baptist History and Heritage* said that Jefferson's Declaration of Independence sounded "strangely" like Williams.[55] That statement is one of profound significance.

What we do know is that Jefferson often said the Declaration of Independence was "an expression of the American mind." Certainly by 1776, the colonists were reading John Locke and others like him. Liberty was already the epitome of the "American mind."

How did the American mind reject the *Old World Order*?

A Most Humble Supplication (1620)

---

[54] Appleton's American Encyclopedia, Vol. II, 293.

[55] Joseph Martin Dawson, "Roger Williams or John Locke?", *Baptist History and Heritage*, October, 1966, 13.

We last left the Puritans in our briefing while they were beating Obadiah Holmes and hanging Quakers for violating their religious establishment. What changed the American mind between 1651 and 1776? Our answer: The Baptist principles of *equality before God* and *liberty of conscious*. These *American principles*, did not originate in the *Age of Enlightenment*, but in the dungeons and martyrs' fires of the *Old World Order*. Even the phrases of the Declaration came from an earlier source than Locke.

Chapter two of our briefing closed with the plea of Leonard Busher for his religious liberty. His plea was unanswered, but it began a series of writings that changed the minds of the greatest thinkers in English history.

According to the *Old World Order*, dissenters were so pernicious that not only were their bodies destroyed, but their wicked thoughts as well. Consequently, their works, as we have discussed, were systematically destroyed.

However, in the sixteenth century a few writings began to emerge. The world has a record of Baptist dissent in England beginning in the mid-sixteenth century with the views of John Wycliff, the Lollard.

Honest historians admit that the Lollards, rejecting infant baptism for believer's baptism were indeed Baptist. Wycliff's writings, escaping the destruction of the *Old World Order*, represented the first stone in the building of the *separation* of God's people from the world.

An era of writing upon the subject of liberty began to illuminate Europe and especially England. Every Baptist Christian should become familiar with the classic book, *Tracts on the Liberty of Conscious*. "Tracts" included writings from 1614-1661, and was compiled by Edward Bean Underhill.

Beginning with Wycliff, a three hundred-year battle for the mind of Europe was waged from the dirty prisons of the European continent and the British Isles.

By far the most important petition was *A Most Humble Supplication*, written in 1620 by an anonymous Baptist imprisoned in the Newgate Prison of London.

Sometime in the years of his confinement, the anonymous prisoner at Newgate began an extraordinary defense of Baptist principles and civil liberty. Not only was the content extraordinary, but also the fashion in which it was written. The prisoner had to smuggle his writings on parchments stuffed into milk bottles. The message itself was written in milk. It could only be read by browning the parchment by candle flame. The message then was transcribed. *A Most Humble Supplication* was written in this fashion and submitted to the King of England.

To this day, we do not know the identity of the author of *A Most Humble Supplication*. Apparently he perished in prison. Both King and Parliament ignored his pleas, but the common people heard. And most importantly, the American pioneer preacher, Roger Williams heard. Today, all Americans should be familiar with his words. We will produce some of them here pointing out the principles we all readily accept as part of "the American mind":

To the high and mighty King, James, by the grace of God,

As your majesty well observeth in these words: It is a good and safe rule in theology, that in matters of the worship of God, *quod dubitas, ne feceris*, according to Paul's rule, "**Let every man be fully persuaded in his own mind**." (reason)

It is not in your power to compel the heart; you may compel men to be hypocrites, as a great many are, who are false-hearted both towards God and the state; which is sin both in you and them. **The vileness of persecuting the body of any man, only for**

cause of conscience, is against the word of God and law of Christ. (no punishment to so-called heretics)

Let the wheat and tares grow together in the world, until the harvest. (soul liberty)

CHAPTER I. The rule of faith is the doctrine of the Holy Ghost contained in the sacred scriptures.

Much by us shall not need to be written on this subject, **the thing is so evident, and so generally acknowledged, at least in words**. (self-evident truth in the minds of Christian people)

Common sense teacheth, that he which is a party, cannot be judge. (reason and trial by jury of your peers)

CHAPTER IV. Those that fear and obey God, and so have the Spirit of God to search out and know the mind of God in the scriptures, are commonly, and for the most part, the simple, poor, despised.

Proved, our Saviour saith, The poor receive the gospel; (all men equal)

The truth of this is as plain as may be, that **the scriptures being the rule of faith**, perfect and absolute, and that the plainness of them is such, **as by the Spirit of God they may be easily understood of those that fear and obey God**. (individualism)

Which is also confirmed by human testimonies. (experience)

The protestants confess, that "in the primitive church, the doctrines and several points of religion, were known and discoursed by the meanest of people, and the bishops exhorted them thereunto. This rule is of that nature, that **it is able to direct any man, be he never so simple**." (individualism, natural law, and men are created equal)

Chrysostom: "The scriptures are easy to understand, and exposed to the capacity of **every servant and ploughman, and widow, and boy, and him that is most unwise**." (all men equal)

And what is more frequent in the mouths of many protestants, yea, the bishops themselves, that these and such like words: "**Must every base fellow, cobbler, tailor weaver, &c. meddle with the exposition or discoursing of the scriptures**, which appertain to none but to the learned? (all men have a "right" to read the scriptures and learn)

58

Thus are here sufficient testimonies **proved from scriptures and experience**, that the learned may, and have usually erred. (experience)[56]

The Bloudy Tenet of Persecution (1644)

Someone would make the world know of the plea for liberty from the anonymous prisoner at Newgate. His name was Roger Williams. Here is a quick summary of the life of the man many historians refer to as "the first American:"

- Roger Williams was born in 1599.
- He was educated at Oxford. Williams worked for Sir Edward Coke in 1620.
- He married Mary Barnard in 1629.
- He came to America in February of 1631
- Banished from Massachusetts in 1636 for "new and dangerous opinions." One year later, his associate in the founding of Rhode Island, Dr. John Clarke, was also banished.
- A list of Williams' *New and Dangerous* opinions:
  a)He rejected the "Oath of the Freeman" because it declared allegiance to a government married to a church.
  b)He rejected the "Divine Rights of Kings" criticized the confiscating of land belonging to native Americans (the first to record such a protest.)
  c)Mr. Williams preaching and insistence on the hated idea of **LIBERTY OF CONSCIENCE**. He argued against enforcement of the "**First table of the Law,**" the first four commandments or man's personal responsibilities to God.
- Williams wrote the *Bloudy Tenet of Persecution* in 1644.

---

[56] Edward Bean Underhill, *Tracts on the Liberty of Conscience and Persecution, 1614-1661*, (reprint: Elibron Classics series), 189-231.

- He had a wonderful relationship with the native Americans. He was the first missionary to them, one decade ahead of John Elliot.
- A year after the Massachusetts court banished him, they solicited his help to bring about an Indian alliance.
- With John Clarke, 1651-1673, he fought to established the charter of Rhode Island.

The Bloudy Tenet of Persecution, was one of most important literary works of colonial America. It is here that we find the light of liberty shining first from our shores. In it, Roger Williams defended the arguments of the "anonymous prisoner at Newgate" and expressed them in terms very familiar to "the American mind."

Compare the thoughts of Willliams, influenced by the Baptist prisoner of Newgate with Jefferson's **first principles of the American republic**, immortalized in the Declaration of Independence:

American principles certainly did not originate with Augustinian theologians such as Martin Luther or John Calvin. The principles of "the American mind" in 1776, stood in stark opposition to the *Old World Order*. Stigmatizing the Declaration of Independence might indicate residual affection for religious establishment and advocacy of its twin principle: persecution.

First, whereas they say, **that the Civill order may erect and establish what forme of civill Government may seeme in wisedome most meet,** I acknowledge the proposition to be **most true, both in itself,** and also considered with the end of it, that a civill Government is an Ordinance of God, to conserve the civill peace of people, so farre as concernes **their Bodies and Goods,** as formerly hath beene said.

But from the Grant I infer, (as before hath been touched) that the Soveraigne, originall, and **foundation of civill power lies in the people,** (whom they must needs meane by the civill power distinct from the Government set up.) And if so, that **a People may erect and establish what forme of Government seemes to them most meete** for their civill condition: **It is evident** that such Governments as are by them erected and established, **have no more power, nor for no longer time, then the civill power or people consenting and agreeing shall betrust them with.** This is cleere not only in **Reason,** but in the **experience** of all common-weales, where the people are not deprived of their naturall freedome by the power of Tyrants.

We hold these truths to be **self-evident,** that **all men are created equal,** that they are endowed by their Creator with certain **unalienable Rights, that among these are Life, Liberty and the pursuit of Happiness.**--That to secure these rights, Governments are instituted among Men, **deriving their just powers from the consent of the governed,** -- That whenever any Form of Government becomes destructive of these ends, **it is the Right of the People to alter or to abolish it, and to institute new Government,** laying its foundation **on such principles** and organizing its powers **in such form, as to them shall seem most likely to effect their Safety and Happiness.**

Clearly, America's founding principles did not originate with John Locke. Locke only expressed what Baptists had been pleading for hundreds of years.

American principles certainly did not originate with Augustinian theologians such as Martin Luther or John Calvin. The principles of "the American mind" in 1776, stood in stark opposition to the *Old World Order*. Stigmatizing the Declaration of Independence might indicate residual affection for religious establishment and advocacy of its twin principle: persecution.

Certain members of the Reformed Religious Right have little regard for Thomas Jefferson, the author of the Declaration. Perhaps Jefferson's affection for the Baptists has something to do with it. Baptists were civil examples for him. Consider this often repeated testimony concerning Jefferson's affection for Baptist polity. Thomas Armitage wrote:

> There was a small Baptist Church which held its monthly meetings for business at a short distance from Mr. Jefferson's house…Mr. Jefferson attended these meetings for several months in succession. The pastor on one occasion asked him how he was pleased with their church government. Mr. Jefferson replied, that **it struck him with great force** and had interested him much, that **he considered it the only form of true democracy then existing in the world**, and had concluded that **it would be the best plan of government** for the American colonies. This was several years before the Declaration of Independence.[57]

We must remember that not only did the Baptists express the principles of life and liberty, they put those principles into practice in a "lively experiment." Roger Williams, along with Dr. John Clarke, established the first government in the world with religious and civil

---

[57] Thomas Armitage, *History of the Baptists, vol. 2* (New York: Bryan, Taylor and Co., 1890), 734.

liberty in Rhode Island. This government stood in opposition to John Winthrop's state-church marriage in Massachusetts. I. B. Richman wrote:

> Against the somber background of early New England, two figures stand above the rest—John Winthrop and Roger Williams. The first—astute, reactionary, stern—represented Moses and the law. The second—spontaneous, adaptable, forgiving—represented Christ and the individual. It is needless to say with which lay the promise and the dawn.[58]

Bancroft, the great secular historian of the nineteenth century, who is often quoted by catholic Reformed historians such as John Eidsmoe and David Barton, wrote:

> ... when England was gasping under the despotism of intolerance; almost **half a century before William Penn** became an American proprietary; and **two years before** Descartes founded modern philosophy on the method of free reflection, **Roger Williams** asserted the great doctrine of intellectual liberty. It became his glory to found a state upon that principle ... The principles which he first sustained... he soon found occasion to publish to the world, and to defend as **the basis of the religious freedom of mankind;**[59]

Even Gary North, catholic Reformed Presbyterian writer said this about Rhode Island:

> The political history of the United States after 1689 has essentially been the extension of Roger Williams' view of civil government, as opposed to John Winthrop's.[60]

---

[58] Irving Bernine Richman, *Rhode Island, Its Making And Its Meaning* (**Providence, RI:** G. P. Putnam's Sons, 1902). and Arthur B. Strickland, *Roger Williams* (Boston: The Judson Press, 1919), 80.

[59] George Bancroft, *History of the United States, vol. 1* (Boston: Little, Brown, and Co., 1879) 297-8.

[60] Gary North, *Political Polytheism* (Tyler, TX: Institute for Christian Economics, 1989), 315.

Acknowledgement of the Baptist expression of principles in the American Republic is not a new contention. Even though Roger Williams did not remain a Baptist, nor did he begin the first Baptist church, he will always be associated with the baptized believers, and his writings contain the principles of Baptist Christian Heritage. Historians and concerned citizens did not easily forget Williams' contribution.

In 1872, the Congress of the United States placed a statue of Roger Williams, Baptist defender of both religious and civil liberty in the national capitol. Republican Senator, Henry Anthony, provided the official dedication. It read in part:

> In all our history no name shines with a purer light than his whose memorial we have lately placed in the Capital. In the history of all the world there is no more striking example of a man grasping a grand idea, at once, in its full proportions, and all the completeness, and carrying it out, unflinchingly, to its remotest legitimate results. **Roger Williams did not merely lay the foundations of religious freedom, he constructed the whole edifice**, in all its impregnable strength, and in all its imperishable beauty...Religious freedom, which now, by general consent, underlies the foundation principles of civilized government.[61]

Historians and concerned citizens did not easily forget Dr. John Clarke either. Clarke spent 12 years in England, wrestling with governor Coddington over the

---

[61] Thomas Armitage, *History of the Baptists, vol. 2* (New York: Bryan, Taylor and Co., 1890), 644-645.

state of Rhode Island. He won independence for his state and wrote the Rhode Island Charter. The Charter was widely recognized as a model for the U.S. Constitution, before pagan and Reformed re-writers banished it into obscurity. In Providence, on the west facade of the capital building is engraved the immortal words of Dr. Clarke:

...A MOST FLOURINGING CIVIL STATE MAY STAND AND BEST BE MAINTAINED AND THAT AMONG OUR ENGLISH SUBJECTS, WITH A FULL LIBERTY IN RELIGIOUS CONCERNMENTS.
—JOHN CLARKE

The courageous principles of the pioneers of liberty, Roger Williams and Dr. John Clarke received the respect and admiration of the entire world.

Non-Baptist American historians of the past had much to say about the Baptists, their doctrine of religious liberty, and their contribution to American liberty:

> Thus for the first time in history, a form of government (Rhode Island) was adopted which drew a clear and unmistakable line between the temporal and the spiritual power, and **a community came into being which was an anomaly among the nations**.
> —Prof. J. L. Diman.[62]

No one principle of political or social or religious policy lies nearer the base of American institutions and has done more to shape our career than this principle inherited from Rhode Island, and it may be

---

[62] Arthur B. Strickland, *Roger Williams* (Boston: The Judson Press, 1919), 28.

asserted that the future of America was in a large measure determined by that General Court which summoned Roger Williams to answer for "divers new and dangerous opinions," and **his banishment became a pivotal act in universal history.**—Prof. Alonzo Williams.[63]

In the code of laws established by them, [Clarke and Williams] we read for the first time since Christianity ascended the throne of the Caesars, the declaration **that conscience should be free and men should not be punished for worshiping God in the way they were persuaded He requires.**—Judge Story.[64]

In the seventeenth century there was no place but the wilderness for such a John the Baptist of the distant future as Roger Williams. He did not belong among the diplomatic builders of churches, like Cotton, or the political founders of States, like Winthrop. He was but a babbler to his own time, but **the prophetic voice rings clear and far, and ever clearer as the ages go on.**—Edward Eggleston[65]

It should be noted by every patriotic American, especially every Baptist Christian, that Rhode Island became the haven of refuge for the hated of this world. From the Quakers to the Huguenots, the disfranchised came. Fittingly, the children of the Diaspora of Israel came. It should be no surprise that the first freely operating Jewish Synagogue in the West was established a few hundred feet from the First Baptist Church in America, Clarke Memorial Baptist Church in Newport, Rhode Island. Therefore, it should not surprise us that Hebrew scholars, God's Old Covenant children, should have respect for the Baptists. In 1912, Rabbi Abram

---

[63] Ibid.

[64] Ibid.

[65] Edward Eggleston, *The Beginners of a Nation* (New York: D. Appleton & Co., 1897), 80.

Simon, Ph.D., in an address to the Reformed Congregation Keneseth Israel, Philadelphia, said:

...we point to the great principles of equal and religious freedom, written into the Constitution of forty-eight States, and **engraven on the minds** of ninety millions of people in our country and making their moral and civic influence felt all over the civilized globe, as worthy tributes to the genius of Roger Williams.[66]

In 1919, the Hon. Oscar S. Straus, twice American Ambassador to Turkey, Secretary of Labor, and Commerce in the late President Roosevelt's Cabinet, and President of the League to Enforce Peace, on the eve of sailing for Europe and the Peace Conference said:

...if I were asked whom to hold before the American people and the world **to typify the American spirit of fairness, of freedom, of liberty in Church and State, I would without any hesitation select ... the great and immortal Roger Williams.** He became a Baptist...a community and a church which is famous for never having stained its hands with the blood of persecutors.[67]

Do you still doubt that the Baptists were used of God to be the architects of religious and governmental liberty in the world? Would you believe the testimony of the Prime Minister of Britain, David Lloyd-George? Lloyd-George faced the German Army during World War I. He understood the oppression and tyranny of the *Old World Order.*

---

[66] Arthur B. Strickland, *Roger Williams, Prophet and Pioneer of Soul Liberty* (Boston: The Judson Press, 1919), ix.

[67] Idid., xiv.

Lloyd-George sent this startling message[68] to the American National Baptist convention of 1918:

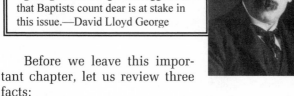

> **It is Baptist principles that we are fighting for** in this great struggle. All that Baptists count dear is at stake in this issue.—David Lloyd George

Before we leave this important chapter, let us review three facts:

1. Not so long ago, Baptist historians understood that American principles were basically Baptist principles.

2. Not so long ago, secular historians understood that American principles were basically Baptist principles.

3. Not so long ago, even Hebrew scholars understood that American principles were basically Baptist principles.

These all understood the "American mind" and were impressed with the blessings that came upon our wonderful country and to the entire world.

However, not everyone was impressed.

---

[68] George Coleman, President, Northern Baptist Convention, speech at Atlantic City, N.J., May, 1918.

Chapter 8
Samuel Rutherford v. American Principles

We continue the third part of our briefing. As we have stated, **the third ax blow laid to Baptist roots is the Christian educational system**. It has severed us from our American principles. More background is needed to bring our reader up to speed.

The Baptists are marked. Not by the mark of antichrist, but marked for death by the spirit of antichrist and the coming *New World Order*. During the dark ages, the spirit of antichrist had a thousand year reign. The actual and literal person of the Beast (antichrist) will reign on this earth for seven more years.

> But we intended good to men, not to sects. The not burning of the Samaritans doth prove nothing for the immunity of hereticks from the sword.
>
> — Samuel Rutherford (in answer to Roger Williams' plea for religious liberty.)

This is in fulfillment of the book of Revelation. This is not an interpretation, it is the result of viewing the scriptures as being literally true. This fundamentally separates the Augustinian Worldview from the Pauline/Baptist Worldview. The martyrs in Revelation will be Baptist in principle, as they will never receive the "mark" of the Beast. Our Baptist forefathers recognized that "mark" as infant baptism. Oh, how they suffered because of infant baptism, the initiation into Mother Church!

A new initiation is coming. And Baptist people will dissent, and they will be butchered again. Note this vile statement from a "Covenanter" website:

Baptists fought against theocracy and ushered in a golden age of anti-covenantal pluralism.[69] Any time you have a union of Church and State, Baptists tend to be...persecuted. Translation: Don't try to apply God's law to civil government because baptists [sic] will rebel against it and be punished for their rebellion. Always glad to clarify. Study the history of Anabaptism, and you'll see that very little has changed in 500 years.[70]

I am not saying that all catholic Reformed share the view of the above, but their theology is paving the way for such monstrous behavior.

The Devil has his own conspiracy and the catholic Reformed are ignorantly aiding in it.

The experiment of Clarke and Williams in Rhode Island was considered dangerous and could not go unchallenged.

Williams' *Bloody Tenet of Persecution*, because of its insistence on religious and civil liberty, and because of its popularity, threatened the power structure of the *Old World Order*. When it was first published in 1644, *The Bloudy Tenet* was publicly burned, and Williams was defamed.

John Cotton gave his answer from Massachusetts. Others would challenge the dangerous notion of liberty as well.

The Scottish Presbyterian minister, Samuel Rutherford, answered Williams with *A Free Disputation Against Pretended Liberty of Conscience* in 1649.

The grossly overrated Rutherford did his best to answer Williams. As one of the "divines" who oversaw the Westminster Confession of Faith of 1646, Samuel Rutherford was at least well versed in the proper Presbyterian relationship within the church and state marriage.

---

[69] He is referring to the American War of Independence.

[70] http://www.littlegeneva.com/?m=200207

In 1644, the same year Roger Williams published his *Bloody Tenet of Persecution*, Samuel Rutherford introduced *Lex, Rex* (The Law and the Prince). Rutherford dismissed the *Divine Rights of Kings* doctrine, as did Williams. But that is where their similarities end. Rutherford replaced the *Divine Rights of Kings* with the *Divine Right of the Presbytery* doctrine. The Presbyterian Church was to have control of the church-state marriage.

In *Lex, Rex*, Rutherford insisted the magistrate is entrusted with enforcing *both tables* of the ten commandments. This is contrary to Williams' contention that the first four commandments are items of the conscience and cannot be enforced by civil law. Rutherford, as a member of the *Old World Order*, argued maintenance of religion by the power of the sword. From Rutherford's *Lex, Rex*:

> Kings and magistrates are God's, and God's deputies and lieutenants upon earth (Psalm 82:1, 6, 7; Exod. 22:8; 4:16)...and their throne is the throne of God, I Chron. 22:10 (Question III. 4).

> Magistrates (not the king only but all the princes of the land) and judges are to maintain religion by their commandments and to take care of religion (Question XIV. Assert.1).[71]

Samuel Rutherford wrote directly against Roger Williams, John Clarke and the Baptists in his *A Free*

---

[71] http://www.constitution.org/sr/lexrex.htm

Disputation Against Pretended Liberty of Conscience (1649):

Whether peace of civil societies be sure, **where there is toleration of all Religions**, and **what peace Christians can have in Toleration?**

Peace is commanded in the new Testament, no word of toleration of divers [diverse] Religions, which are the Seminaries of discords between the seed of the woman and the Serpents seed, in all the New Testament, is to be found by precept, promise, or practice, nor any ground of repealing judicial Lawes, for punishing seducing Teachers.

Libertines [he means those who contend for liberty of conscience] allege, Luke 9:51,52,53, &c. When Christ by a village of the Samaritans, was dejected and denied, James and John say, "Lord, wilt thou that we command fire come downe from heaven, and consume them, even as Elias did?" But Christ rebuked them and said, "ye know not what manner of spirit ye are of, for the Son of man is not to come to destroy mens lives, but to save them." Then are we to spare the lives of those that refuse the true and sound doctrine of the Gospel, yea who oppugne it...?

The not burning of the Samaritans doth prove nothing for the immunity of hereticks from the sword.

...(but we intended good to men, not to sects) endeavouring of nearest uniformity in the three Kingdomes, which we did sweare is contrary to actuall tollerating of all sects and Religions, but the Sectaries endeavour the latter, and have compassed it, ergo, the Sectaries are gone contrary to their Oath and Covenant.

The word of God as it is in every man's conscience [is] no rule of Reformation in the Covenant.[72]

For anyone familiar with the Religious Right, the *Rutherford Institute* has been a stalwart in the so-called culture war for "Biblical principles." Why would John Whitehead, a leader in the Religious Right, name his

---

[72] http://www.swrb.com/newslett/actualNLs/ruthrefwil.htm

legal defense organization after the persecuting Samuel Rutherford?

Although Whitehead has distanced himself from them, his writings are a part of the catholic Reformed *Reconstructionist* movement. Whitehead successfully changed Christian opinion on the subject of liberty and the separation of church and state with his 1977 book, *The Separation Illusion.* R. J. Rushdoony wrote the foreword.

Somehow, in this 209 page book on the all important principle of religious liberty through separation of the state from the church, Roger Williams' name is only mentioned once. None of his principles (or the principles of the Baptists) are discussed.

For the record, Roger Williams never advocated separating God from society, he recognized that government consisted of people from society. His principles stated what Baptist Christian prisoners had proclaimed, that government had to secure consent from the rest of society to govern. It follows that if Christian people permeated society, government would be just. Therefore, in order to have truly Christian government, society needed salvation, (revival and awakening) not coercion from a theocratic state. That is why Williams and company stood for *disestablishment* of church-state theocracies. It was a courageous stand in his day.

Today, the *Reconstructionists* teach that the separation of the church from the state is an *illusion.* Some have called for the re-establishment of the church-state marriage.

To make it happen, these self-proclaimed enemies of the Baptists have been influencing our children for over 30 years. We will explore this outrageous fact, but first we need to become better acquainted with the absurdity of catholic Reformed *Reconstructionist* ideas.

Chapter 9
The catholic Reformed v. American Principles

In case you believe that the likes of Samuel Rutherford are simply a part of *The Old World Order*, you may be surprised at what you are about to read.

American history has been intentionally hidden and rewritten. Very few have knowledge of the founding principles of American liberty.

Liberty had enemies when she arose from the dungeons and she still has those enemies today. One place to find such enemies is to visit **www.freebooks.com.**

This is a website developed by Gary North, the son-in-law of Rousas J. Rushdoony. It contains free downloads of thousands of pages of the political and theological writings of the catholic Reformed.

Their main target to this day is the Baptists. If you don't believe me, just go to freebooks.com and download *The Failure of American Baptist Culture*. This was the first of their books stating their position on the culture war.

I promise if you are a patriotic Baptist Christian, you will not believe what you will read. Let me provide you with a few choice quotes:

On free expression:
  When someone makes his conscience public, and leads others into idolatry, blasphemy, adultery, and other such things, I think its become more than a private opinion. He's promoting new public policy. And that, I think, should be stopped.—Craig Bulkeley[73]

---

[73] Craig Bulkeley, "Christianity and Religious Liberty," *The Failure of the American Baptist Culture* (Tyler, TX: Geneva Divinity School, *Christianity and Civilization, Vol. 1*, 1982), 248.

On religious liberty:
Some call it "religious liberty," others call it "liberty of conscience," I call it trouble.—Craig S. Bulkeley[74]

On religious liberty:
The religious liberty/liberty of conscience philosophy of religion is contradictory and unbiblical.—Craig Bulkeley[75]

On religious liberty:
When the "liberty of conscience/religious liberty" idea is allowed to run its full course it leads inevitably to dissent and social disintegration.—Craig Bulkeley[76]

On the Trinity, Salvation and Authority:
You see if we really push the matter, then Baptists disagree with catholics [catholic Reformed] over such fundamental issues as the Trinity, the nature of salvation, and even the nature of Biblical authority.
—James B. Jordan[77]

On the rights of individuals:
The idea of rights is the outgrowth of theories of government from Enlightenment humanism. T.R. Ingram has countered the notion that men, simply because they are men, have certain "inalienable rights." "Human rights."
—Kevin Craig[78]

On the rights of individuals:
Perhaps another observation can be made, to illustrate the differences between Reformed and Baptistic thinking. That is the matter of human rights. Is the catholic and Reformed

---

[74] Ibid., 244.

[75] Ibid., 271.

[76] Ibid., 262.

[77] James B. Jordan, *The Failure of the American Baptist Culture* (Tyler, TX: Geneva Divinity School, *Christianity and Civilization, Vol. 1,* 1982), x.

[78] Kevin Craig, "Social Apologetics," *The Failure of the American Baptist Culture* (Tyler, TX: Geneva Divinity School, *Christianity and Civilization, Vol. 1,* 1982), 50.

faith opposed to human rights? Yes, very much so.—James B. Jordan[79]

On the rights of individuals:
The human rights idea has been cried up for an alternative to Divine law as the basis and foundation of government ever since the Declaration of Rights of Virginia in 1776. It is a foundation of sand.—T. R. Ingram[80]

On Roger Williams and individual rights:
Williams and his followers, and for that matter all those who support the "religious liberty" idea, all embrace the religion of Deism in principle and practice, if not also in name.—Craig Bulkeley[81]

On Rhode Island and its government:
It was against the Puritans' vision of a New Israel in the New England wilderness that the citizens of Rhode Island rebelled, and in doing so, they led the world, step by step, into a political conspiracy against God.—Gary North[82]

On Baptist heritage:
Baptist history, theology, and sociology must be presented. Its underlying presuppositions are devastating to civilization.—Ray Sutton[83]

On the future of the Baptists:

---

[79] James B. Jordan, *The Failure of the American Baptist Culture* (Tyler, TX: Geneva Divinity School, *Christianity and Civilization, Vol. 1*, 1982), xi.

[80] T. R. Ingram, "What's wrong with human rights?" *The Theology of Christian Resistance* (Tyler, TX: Geneva Divinity School, *Christianity and Civilization, Vol. 2*, 1983), 133.

[81] Craig Bulkeley, "Christianity and Religious Liberty," *The Failure of the American Baptist Culture* (Tyler, TX: Geneva Divinity School, *Christianity and Civilization, Vol. 1*, 1982), 256.

[82] Gary North, *Political Polytheism* (Tyler, TX: Institute for Christian Economics, 1989), inside dusk jacket.

[83] Ray Sutton, "The Baptist Failure," *The Failure of the American Baptist Culture* (Tyler, TX: Geneva Divinity School, *Christianity and Civilization, Vol. 1*, 1982), 152.

Baptist history, theology and sociology spell failure. The system at root centers around man. For that reason the American Baptist paradigm will go the way of man—death.
–Ray Sutton[84]

---

[84] Ibid., 184.

Chapter 10
The Strange World of Gary North

Today, the Reformed try to distance themselves from the radical *Reconstructionists*. My guess is that Roujas Rushdoony and Gary North are just so controversial, they make for bad press. Gary North apparently ruined his credibility during the Y2K scare. During Y2K, North had thousands, perhaps millions purchasing his survival kits, generators and various and sundry materials. All of the Christian media celebrities were pointing people to his website. Some veterans of *Reconstructionism*, such as William Einwechter and Gary DeMar still quote him. Here are some of North's more outrageous ideas:

> ...the U.S. Constitution is judicially anti-Christian. It is an explicitly covenantal document; it is also explicitly not Christian. It was designed that way. But if it is not Christian, then it must be anti-Christian...What Madison and the Framers proposed was a revolutionary break from the history of mankind's governments, with only one glaring exception: the state of Rhode Island... the Framers adopted it as the judicial foundation of the proposed national government.[85]

> A handful of men had decided to take the new nation down a different path. They wanted a completely new system of national government. This would have to be achieved through a coup...It required, in short, a conspiracy.[86]

> James Madison was a covenant-breaking genius, and the heart and soul of his genius was his commitment to religious neutralism. He devised a Constitution that for two centuries has fooled even the most perceptive Christian social phi-

---

[85] Gary North, *Political Polytheism*, (Tyler, TX: Institute for Christian Economics, 1989), 380.

[86] Ibid., 416.

losophers of each generation into thinking that Madison was not what he was: a Unitarian theocrat whose goal was to snuff out the civil influence of the Trinitarian churches whenever they did not support his brainchild. For two centuries, his demonic plan has worked.[87]

Madison is often called the Father of the Constitution. It was surely Madison who was the father of the Convention, with Washington sitting silently as the godfather.[88]

The conspirators knew it, especially the man who made the coup possible, George Washington.[89]

When the [Constitutional] Convention ended, they took the final step. They handed all the minutes over to George Washington to take back to Mount Vernon. They knew that no one in the nation would have the audacity to tell George Washington that he had to hand over the evidence of what was in fact a coup.[90]

There is no escape from this conclusion: the United States Constitution is an atheistic, humanistic covenant.[91]

The Federalist Papers were propaganda devices to persuade the voters retroactively to sanction the coup of 1787...Once sanctioned by the ratification process, the original conspirators became, retroactively, Founding Fathers. The fact that it was a coup was concealed to the general public. The victors and their allies wrote the textbooks.[92]

In order to make the results of their closed-door conspiracy sound more authoritative and legitimate, the conspirators added these three words in the Preamble: "We the People." Democracy literally means "people's rule." The sover-

---

[87] Ibid., 696.
[88] Ibid., 428.
[89] Ibid.
[90] Ibid., 418.
[91] Ibid., 403.
[92] Ibid., 419.

eignty of the people is the basis of the modern democratic order.[93]

The question of resistance to tyranny is not simply hypo-thetical. Lawyer John Whitehead discusses the rivalry be-tween statist religion and biblical religion. The Bible author-izes resistance against an unlawful self-deifying state when that state transgresses biblical law.[94]

To undermine a society, its opponents must first under-mine men's faith in the existing moral and philosophical foundations of the society.[95]

James Madison and the Framers put forth a new national covenant based on William's model in 1787, and the voters' representatives ratified it in 1788. We live under its jurisdic-tion still. We will not live under it forever.[96]

Politically, the only legitimate long-term biblical goal is the creation of a worldwide theocratic republic.[97]

In the fall of 1982, I was invited to meet in Virginia Beach, Virginia, with Pat Robertson, who heads "The 700 Club" and the Christian Broadcasting Network. He wanted suggestions about what needed to be done to reverse the drift into hu-manism by the United States. Also invited were Francis Schaeffer, his son Franky, and John Whitehead, the lawyer who specializes in defending Christian causes. I met Schaeffer twice, the first time in late 1963 or early 1964 in the den of Rev. Richard Gray in Pennsylvania where he dis-cussed his ministry with a few seminarians, and again in late 1982 at a private meeting at Pat Roberstson's Virginia Beach headquarters, Rev. Robertson had invited me,

---

[93] Ibid., 647.

[94] Gary North, *The Theology of Christian Resistance* (Tyler, TX: Geneva Divinity School, *Christianity and Civilization, Vol. 2*, 1983), xxi.

[95] Gary North, *Conspiracy, A Biblical View* (Tyler, TX: Dominion Press, 1986), 41.

[96] Gary North, *Political Polytheism* (Tyler, TX: Institute for Christian Economics, 1989), 371.

[97] Ibid., 650.

Schaeffer, Franky, and lawyer John Whitegead to advise him regarding programs that CBN University could launch. I wrote a paper for him which was later published as "Levers, Fulcrums, and Hornets," As far as I know, Rev. Robertson never adopted any of our suggestions. Rev. Falwell did; his Liberty University's videotape-based home college education program was developed after Falwell's assistant, Ron Godwin, read the essay and adopted its educational strategy.[98]

We have one more piece of information for this chapter.

I wrestled with including parts of *A Presbyterian Political Manifesto* in this briefing. The so-called manifesto is posted at various places on the internet. The author of the manifesto is not a fringe figure, but a respected doctor of theology. His writings have appeared in the *Chalcedon Report* and *Reformed Perspective*. The following quote will to show you the seriousness of the *Reconstructionists*. Notice that **Samuel Rutherford, Rousas John Rushdoony and Gary North** are quoted.

A PRESBYTERIAN POLITICAL MANIFESTO: PRESBYTERIANISM AND CIVIL GOVERNMENT by Michael Wagner, 1997.

For the last two decades or so there has been an apparent increase in the amount of conservative Christian political activism in North America. Many evangelicals and fundamentalists who had previously shunned politics began to see the necessity of political participation in order to prevent the encroachment of the state upon their legitimate activities, such as Christian education, or to prevent national sins, such as legalized abortion.

It is this author's settled conviction that the Westminster Confession of Faith is the most accurate and thoroughgoing account of the doctrines of God's inerrant Word, and is therefore the most reasonable choice for a Christian state to adopt. It is the contention of this paper that the historic Presbyterian view

---

[98] Ibid., 176.

of the necessity for **the establishment of Presbyterianism as the official religion of every society is the Scriptural view**.

Human societies are characterized by a common religious foundation which provides cohesion and a basis for law. **R.J. Rushdoony** has done much to bring this to light.

[As Rushdoony wrote], "no disestablishment of religion as such is possible in any society"

The liberty and prosperity that we still (decreasingly) enjoy are residuals from an implicit Christian foundation that is quickly being eroded and replaced by **the religion of secular humanism.**

The Bible does indeed demonstrate the need for **an establishment of Christianity**, and the Old Testament in particular provides the Biblical basis for the concept of an established church.

Would people of other religions or different Christian sects be allowed to freely exercise their beliefs? Westminster Confession of Faith, Chapter 20, "Of Christian Liberty, and Liberty of Conscience." Section 4 ...they who, upon pretence of Christian liberty, shall oppose any lawful power, or the lawful exercise of it, whether it be civil or ecclesiastical, resist the ordinance of God. And for their publishing of such opinions, or maintaining of such practices, ...may lawfully be called to account, and proceeded against by the censures of the church, and by the power of the civil magistrate.

As **Samuel Rutherford** puts it, the civil ruler is "to preserve **both tables of the law**," i.e., all ten of the commandments (Exodus 20: 1 - 17; Deuteronomy 5: 6 - 21).

But some words from **Gary North** are appropriate here. I am not writing a manifesto to be used in today's elections. I am writing a manifesto for the more distant future.

Christians need to ensure that their own children are receiving a **Christian education**. Only by raising godly families and evangelizing the lost will the foundation be laid for **the future reconstruction of civil government** along Biblical lines.

Presbyterian Michael Wagner says, "Christians need to ensure that their own children are receiving a Christian education."

Well, are they?

The catholic Reformed *Reconstructionists*, having stated they must reshape the minds of the American people, are in the process doing just that—to your children.

Chapter 11
Reconstruction of the Baptist School Movement

> Thus, **the ideas** of the *Reconstructionists* **have penetrated into Protestant circles that for the most part are unaware of the original source** of the theological ideas that are beginning to transform them.—Gary North[99]

> So let us be blunt about it: we must use the doctrine of religious liberty to gain independence for Christian schools until we train up a generation of people who know that there is no religious neutrality, no neutral law, no neutral education, and no neutral civil government. Then **they will get busy in constructing a Bible-based social, political and religious order which finally denies the religious liberty of the enemies of God.**—Gary North[100]

> We are now in a position to fuse together in a working activist movement the **three major legs of the Reconstructionist movement: the Presbyterian-oriented educators, the Baptist school headmasters and pastors, and the charismatic telecommunications system**. When this takes place, the whole shape of American religious life will be transformed.—Gary North[101]

The question is, "What does *all of this* have to do with **me**?" I believe any conscientious Christian would

---

[99] Gary North, *Unholy Spirits* (Fort Worth: Dominion Press, 1986), 375.

[100] Gary North, *The Failure of the American Baptist Culture* (Tyler, TX: Geneva Divinity School, *Christianity and Civilization, Vol. 1*, 1982) 25.

[101] Gary North, *Backward Christian Soldiers? An Action Manual For Christian Reconstruction* (Tyler, TX: Institute for Christian Economics, 1984), 150.

be concerned about the educational system of several million American Baptist school children.

If you've been educated in the Christian Schools of America you've probably never heard much of Roger Williams, John Clarke, Shubal Stearns, the dissenter prisoners, or the historic Baptist contribution to American liberty. Instead, you probably have heard that American principles are Puritan principles, or Calvinist principles. You probably have been introduced to "conservatism," or the "Biblical Worldview." In a sense, you have been indoctrinated with the *Old World Order*. In some cases you have been subject to deception.

Some of the deception was accidental. Good people with the best intentions work in the Christian School curriculum industry and are sincere dedicated Baptist Christians. But sadly, the evidence suggests that some of the deception was intentional, perpetrated by those who had nothing but bad intentions.

In the beginning years of the Christian School movement, several curriculum took flight. Most notable were the A Beka curriculum from Pensacola, Florida, Bob Jones University Press in Greenville, South Carolina and Accelerated Christian Education, out of Garland, Texas. Sometime after, Alpha-Omega Lifepac systems began and more recently, Landmark's Freedom Baptist Curriculum. Home schools use these materials along with Liberty Christian, or the most prominent home school system, Bill Gothard's ATIA.

Baptist churches led the way in the beginning of the Christian School movement. THE book that launched the movement was *Rebirth of Our Nation*, (originally titled *To Save a Nation*) by Dr. Donald Howard.

Since theology is the engine that runs life, we should have been interested in Dr. Howard's theological engine. And he told us, back in 1976. On page iii, Dr. Howard credits the two men who most influenced his views on Christian education:

When the original manuscript was prepared for *Save a Nation*, it inadvertently went to press with two omissions: **Dr. Rushdoony's Introduction**, and credit to **Dr. Frances Schaeffer** for support material gleaned from his lectures on the various topics covered in this book.[102]

Of course, you should know from our briefing that Rushdoony is the father of the catholic Reformed *Reconstruction* movement. Francis Schaeffer was the leading catholic Reformed Presbyterian philosopher of his day.

Honestly, I do not have a problem if Rousas John Rushdoony or Francis Schaeffer imparts philosophy to a *Presbyterian* School system, because that is what they are. If they had laid the foundation for a nationwide network of catholic Reformed *Reconstructionist* preparatory schools, they would have received no complaint from me. But was it not deceitful that these two Reformed (Augustinian) philosophers sat in on the ground floor of what was definitely a Baptist movement?

Rebirth of Our Nation was released in the early days of the movement and was marketed primarily to Baptist churches. The back cover includes pictures and recommendations from the two most prominent independent Baptist preachers of the time (1976-1979), Dr. Jack Hyles and Dr. Jerry Falwell. Rushdoony had evidently portrayed himself as a great "fundamental" educator.

Here is Mr. Rushdoony's endorsement, written for the back cover, circa 1979:

> **A War is on**, and, if you are unaware of it, you will be on the casualty list of God and man. This war is humanism's war against Christianity...The real division in the church today **in no longer in terms of the old controversies,** [Does Rushdoony mean doctrine, baptism, and the second coming?] but is between

---

[102] Dr. Donald Howard, *Rebirth of Our Nation* (Lewisville, TX: Accelerated Christian Education, 1979.

those who are active in the battle against humanism and those who are not.[103]

"A war is on!" Remember, Rushdoony and company gave us permission to lie, deceive and do whatever is necessary to win a war. Against whom? The HUMANISTS! And in the thinking of the *Reconstructionists*, humanists and Baptists are identical.

"A war is on, and, if you are unaware of it, you will be on the casualty list of God and man. This war is humanism's war against Christianity. In his book, <u>Rebirth of Our Nation</u>, Dr. Donald R. Howard gives us an account of that war, and some battle strategy. Read it, and join the battle. The real division in the church today is no longer in terms of the old controversies, but is between those who are active in the battle against humanism and those who are not. As an active fighter in this battle, Dr. Howard issues a call to action."

Rev. R.J. Rushdoony
The Chalcedon Report

Well, Rushdoony and Schaeffer certainly got Don Howard on board. On page 224 Howard wrote:

A new system of schools and a new curriculum **based on the theology and philosophy of the reformers** is taking root, sprouting and budding in church classrooms across America... **A Christian curriculum based upon the Biblical Theism of the reformers is taking shape** in a form equal to or superior to that of government education and is gaining a quality of credibility against a growing opposition.[104]

On page 103, we learn that America's founding principles originated, not with Roger Williams and the Baptists, but from their avowed enemy, Presbyterian, Samuel Rutherford!:

Samuel Rutherford wrote a titanic book called *Lex Rex*: "Law is King." The premise of his book is God's revelation: because God had spoken in a book, it is possible to have a rule of **LAW** rather than arbitrary absolute. Locke secularized this concept. Jefferson took it from Locke. **Witherspoon**, one of our founding fathers, said that *Lex Rex* had a greater influence on America than any other book outside of the Bible.

---

[103] Ibid., back cover.
[104] Ibid., 224.

This is a principle built into a concrete foundation: **LAW** and Absolutes. Notice again, "certain inalienable rights." Our American culture was built upon that principle. Because God has spoken, absolute law is possible—this is a presupposition. Since law based upon absolutes is possible, therefore, law can be king: *Lex Rex*.[105]

According to ACE's *Rebirth of Our Nation*, the principles of the Declaration originated with the man who argued that heretics like Williams and the Baptists should be put to death!

The Baptists were excluded from all 372 pages of the inaugural book of the Christian School movement. There is no mention of Williams, no mention of John Clarke, the dissenters, the Separate Baptists or John Leland's influence on James Madison. Instead there is glorification of Martin Luther, John Calvin, John Knox and John Witherspoon, all Reformed clergyman. There is no explanation of true religious liberty.

All curriculums from the major Christian school and home school textbook industry have followed suit. All major Christian School and home school curriculum, with a "Biblical Worldview" or "Christian perspective," are to this day, influenced by the catholic Reformed *Reconstructionists*. A few examples follow.

Bob Jones University Press:
The American Republic for Christian School 2nd Ed., 2000

The only mention of the Baptists occurs on page 54:

"Baptists also settled there."

However the authors said this about the Moravians:

"Probably no other Christian group of the colonial era made as great a missionary effort as did the Moravians."

---

[105] Ibid., 103.

The problem with this statement is that the Moravian leader Elder Solle' said this about the Separate Baptists:

> Mr. [Samuel] Harriss, a well-known Baptist of Virginia, visited here to acquaint himself with our doctrine and constitution and to talk with us....**at this time the Baptists are the only ones in the country who go far and wide preaching and caring for souls.**[106]

The only other reference in *The American Republic for Christian Schools* to the Baptists is on page 456 where they are mentioned with a group of denominations. There is no mention of John Clarke and only two mundane paragraphs referring to Roger Williams.

As to Shubal Stearns and the Separate Baptists? Samuel Davis the famed Presbyterian preacher is given credit for the Great Awakening in the South.

United States History for Christian Schools, 2001

Shubal Stearns actually got a mention on page 80. But on page 26-27, Williams is covered in two paragraphs. Instead of reading about John Clarke, the authors repeat the misinformation about Anne Hutchinson. They falsely charge her with antinomianism (just as John Winthrop had) and then give the wrong definition for it.

On page 68 we find the Baptists were simply a part of the English Separatist movement (Whitsittism).

The overall tone of the book is that liberty and the American way of life were passed to us from Martin Luther.

Heritage Studies 2, (2nd Grade level) 1998

Of Roger Williams and his banishment, the text says, page 41, "He moved away because he did not agree with the other preachers."

---

[106] Adelaide L. Fries, M.A., *Notices of the Records of the Moravians in North Carolina* (Raleigh: Edwards and Broughton Printing Co. 1925), 321.

American Government for Christian Schools, 1999

On pages 22-24, the authors simply bring false information to their students when they claim Martin Luther and the Reformation brought about the "the idea of personal liberty."

Page 24—"The Reformation fathered much of the political and social thinking behind American independence."

John Witherspoon, Presbyterian clergyman is given credit for influencing James Madison. No mention of Williams, Isaac Backus or John Leland.

On page 21, this book contains a bogus quote attributed to James Madison. We will explain this error in our next chapter.

> A common problem in Christian School curriculum is confusion between *freedom*, *toleration* and *liberty*. The Pilgrims wanted *freedom* to worship as they pleased and *toleration* for dissenters. The Puritans wanted theocracy under their leadership and persecution for dissenters. The Baptists wanted religious liberty for all. Unfortunately, this puts the Puritans in a bad light.

Alpha-Omega Publications
Civics (High School Level)
Lifepac 7.8

Begins with Augustine and Aquinas and on page 28 they are referred to as Christianity's "two greatest political thinkers." There is no mention of the Baptist struggle for religious liberty.

Lifepac 9.1

Page 15: "The United States is one of the few countries that practices religious **tolerance**." This is incorrect, the U. S. has guaranteed **liberty**. Tolerance implies an establishment. Also on page 15 is the statement, "Today we may have too much freedom." This is a reoccurring theme in Christian school curriculum. This implies that there is a problem with our liberty and something must be done about it.

Social Studies
Lifepac 1003

Page 6-7:"Those who continued to believe such a false idea were called heretics. Some of the major heresies faced by the early church were Gnosticism, **Donatism**, Arianism, Nestorianism, and Monophysitism."

Page 7, on Christianity in the fourth century: "This clergy consisted of the priests who took care of the laity in local parishes, and of the bishops who were selected by the priests to take care of an area, or **diocese**. Each bishop resided in a city known as a **see**." Note: none of this is indicated to be false, or a deviation from the simplicity of the ancient church.

Page 16: The church fathers recognized by this text are Ambrose, Jerome, Augustine, and Gregory the Great. (Gregory is the Pope who ordered the assimilation of the Baptist Christians of Briton into the Roman Catholic Church. When the pastors refused, they were murdered.)

In discussing the dark ages, no testimony of the Donatists, Albigensians, Paulicians or any other Baptist group is mentioned, although several pages tell us of the rise of monasteries.

Lifepac 1004

Page 24 gives some detail on Wycliffe, but fails to mention his rejection of infant baptism. There is much attention to Luther and Calvin, of course. On page 29 we find the strange assertion that "Calvin believed in the separation of church and state." This is no where near being true. The same page says (correctly) "Calvin was the head of a theocracy in Geneva." There is no mention of Calvin's views on Baptists and their doctrines. No attention is given the writings of the Baptists imprisoned for their faith. In fact, there is no Baptist testimony in *any* Alpha-Omega curriculum.

Foundations for Living
Studies in the Christian Worldview
Unit 1 What is a Biblical Worldview?

This unit teaches two worldviews: the Hebrew (Godly) as opposed to the Greek (ungodly) civilization.

Through the Hebrew civilization comes theocracy (good), through the Greek civilization comes democracy (evil humanism). *Dualism*, which catholic Reformed *Reconstructionists* identify as Baptist beliefs, is especially evil. By the way, "worldview" really means "theology," the engine that runs our lives. It is puzzling that Alpha-Omega uses a *mobius* to depict "God" on page 34.

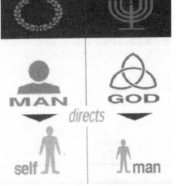

A Beka
America, Land I Love in Christian Perspective, 1994

Much attention is given to the Puritans and Winthrop's City Upon a Hill. Harvard College is featured but no mention of the conversion of its first president, Henry Dunster, to the Baptist faith. (For which he lost his job and nearly his life.)

On page 38 the reoccurring heading, OUR PURITAN HERITAGE is found.

Page 40 gives a fair assessment of Roger Williams, but erroneously credits him with founding the first Baptist church in America.

Page 88 brings a reoccurring figure in Christian School curriculum: Edmund Burke. Burke heavily favored religious establishments in civil government.

Page 97 features the Jewish Patriot Haym Solomon, but it is unfortunate that no histories produced by A Beka record the open door to America provided by the Baptists of Rhode Island.

United States History, Heritage of Freedom, 1996

Page 9 this statement: "The Reformation soon spread throughout Europe, bringing *a revival of Biblical Christianity*, (emphasis theirs) which had been suppressed though never destroyed by leaders of the Roman church throughout the Middle Ages." If the Reformed churches are *Biblical Christianity*, then Baptist churches cannot be.

Pages 33-35 reveal a common problem in Christian School curriculum, confusion between *freedom, toleration* and *liberty*. The Pilgrims wanted *freedom* to worship as they pleased and *toleration* for dissenters. The Puritans wanted theocracy under their leadership and persecution for dissenters. The Baptists wanted religious liberty for all. Unfortunately, that puts the Puritans in a bad light.

Page 37 has the oft-repeated mantra: OUR PURITAN HERITAGE.

Page 38 does give Roger Williams some credit, but page 39 repeats the myth of Anne Hutchinson and does not mention the true hero of the banishment: John Clarke.

Page 55 points out the **Ole Deluder Satan Act**. This "act" is cited in *every* Christian school history. The Massachusetts law of 1642 required towns of 50 or more families to hire a teacher for their children. No one bothers to point out that the children of Baptists (or Quakers) could not attend so they might escape the "Ole Deluder." Nine years after the **Ole Deluder** hit Massachusetts, Obadiah Holmes, and Thomas Painter were beaten half to death for holding Baptist opinions. A number of Quakers were hanged.

Page 57 mentions writings of a religious nature, but no mention of the blockbuster, *Bloudy Tenet of Persecution*.

I am grateful that John Hart and Isaac Backus are mentioned on page 106.

Page 137-139 gives (to my knowledge) the only account of Baptist influence in the foundation of America in any Christian School curriculum. Isaac Backus and John Leland are discussed. There is even a picture of Backus. The piece missing is the Separate Baptist revival under Shubal Stearns and Samuel Harriss, which brought Virginia to the platform of republicanism.

History of our United States (4ᵗʰ Grade) 2003

This text actually mentions Williams, Clarke and the persecution of Obadiah Holmes. This is hopeful, although A Beka's histories still assume "A Puritan Heritage."

Landmark's Freedom Baptist Curriculum
History and Geography H145

Page 30: "The Puritan's were sometimes **hard** on religious nonconformists. Quakers, Baptists, and independent Congregationalists were all expelled from the Colony." The truth is the Puritans disarmed, disfranchised, banished, beat and hung the dissenters.

Page 40 says, "Baptists were quickly outnumbered in Rhode Island..." I am not sure where the author received information for this. Likewise on page 40: "In Georgia, for example, Baptists had freedom of worship, but could not run for office." The truth is that just before the War for Independence, Daniel Marshall (one of the greatest Baptist evangelists and church planters in American history) was arrested in Georgia for preaching the Gospel without Anglican permission.

On page 63 is the familiar claim that **Samuel Rutherford** is somehow responsible for the Declaration of Independence.

Again, there is no mention of Williams, Clarke, Backus, Stearns, the Separate Baptist revival, or John Leland.

Accelerated Christian Education
Social Studies Pace No. 1086, 1990

Martin Luther is given credit for the rise of America on page 4: "It was primarily because of his discovery [referring to justification by faith], the 13 English colonies were established." The omitted truth is that justification by faith was something the Waldensians, Albigensians and Lollards had preached for generations.

Page 17 we find: "The Calvinists in the church [of England] which disagreed ...founded two separate groups: the Puritans and the Separates." This statement perpetuates the idea that Williams, Clarke and the Baptists were simply Calvinists.

Page 25 on Williams: "Gov. Winthrop quietly advised his friend to leave the colony before he could be banished." This is a fictional account. The whole account makes it seem like Williams made his own choice to leave Massachusetts.

Page 25-27 The Pace repeats the misinformation on Anne Hutchinson. Only in this account John Wheelwright, who was the preacher who was banished, is described as one of her followers! There is no mention of the most important person in the banishment, Dr. John Clarke, the founder of the first Baptist church in America.

Social Studies Pace No. 1087, 1990

Under the heading "Birth of Freedom," we learn of the Dutch Reformed, the Moravians (along with the assertion of their evangelistic zeal), the Wesleys, the Presbyterians, the Episcopalians, and the Congregationalist David Brainard.

While we all admire David Brainard, evidence points to the Baptist Christian missionary Isaac McCoy (right), as the greatest American missionary to the Indians. He preached with great power and blessing from 1817-1846, winning Indians and birthing churches all over the Northwest Territory and beyond. McCoy is a non-entry in all Christian School curriculums.

In all these paces, there is no mention of the Baptists, Shubal Stearns, the struggle for liberty, the Gaspee incident, the Regulators, or the Baptist Overmountainmen who fought at Kings Mountain and Cowpens.

Social Studies Pace No. 1088, 1990

This pace reads like it came right out of the book *The Light and the Glory*, by the Presbyterians Peter Marshall and David Manuel. Page 30 concerning the Baptist colony of Rhode Island, the author(s) state: "[Rhode Island] finally decided that it was pointless to remain separate and ratified [the constitution]." There is no mention of the Baptist struggle for the Bill of Rights.

Social Studies Pace No. 1089, 1990

Charles Finney is given attention. Typically, the tremendous church planting and revival of the Separate Baptists of the South during the time of Finney, is not mentioned.

Civics Pace No. 1133, 1997.

This pace begins with the bogus Madison quote about the Constitution, which we will cover in the next chapter.

On page 5 Rousas J. Rushdoony is quoted. On page 10, Augustine is quoted. On page 15, Jerome is quoted. On page 16 the author(s) attempt to blend John Wycliffe and Augustine together. The author(s) also attempt to tie William Tyndale with Zwingli, Luther and Erasmus. Both Wycliffe and Tyndale were Lollards and opposed infant baptism in favor of believer's baptism.

Page 19 has the strange cross-shaped article entitled, "Are you a Protestant?" The word "Baptist" does not appear. I am not sure of the meaning of the article.

Home Schooling?

Jay Rogers wrote, "A little known fact: R. J. Rushdoony, aside from being the founder of Christian *Reconstruction*, is also the founder of the modern home schooling movement."

Is the Home School Legal Defense Association a *Reconstructionist* organization? They definitely embrace the Reformed/*Reconstructionist* worldview. HSLDA has definite ties to the *Reconstructionist* movement through former employees such as attorney Doug Phillips, the son of prominent *Reconstructionist* Howard Phillips, founder of the U.S. Taxpayers Party. HSLDA founder

James Carden was instrumental in introducing the concept of home schooling to Bill Gothard of the Institute in Basic Youth Conflicts.

Bill Gothard's Advanced Training Institute of America

Gothard began his home school program, Advanced Training Institute of America in 1984 and Carden was among the 100 families who piloted the ATIA program.

To any candid observer, Gothard's home school is an advancement of Rushdoony's catholic Reformed *Reconstructionist* views. In ATI the founders of the American republic were catholic Reformed, and nothing about Williams, Clarke, Backus, Leland and the Baptists is mentioned. How can our children know their own heritage and worldview if it is not present in the curriculum?

Christian Liberty Home School

The late Dr. Paul Lindstrom founded and was president of the Christian Liberty Academy Satellite Schools. Christian Liberty is one of the most unabashed proponents of the Reformed *Reconstructionist* worldview.

Of course, we could find little, if any references in *world history* curriculum to the sufferings of Baptist groups such as, the Donatists, Paulicians, Lollards, etc.

Our Conclusion

We conclude that Christian curriculum has severed the Baptist roots of American liberty, and grafted in the pretended roots of covenant theocracy.

This was done according to plan,

It is apparent that the children of one denomination have been reconstructed by a group of educators from another denomination. That denomination **elevates persecutors as heroes**, and, some would argue, operates on the cusp of treason.

END OF PART 3

Epilogue

Epilogue
Chapter 12
David Barton's Omissions

> To Roger Williams and the historic Baptist de-
> nomination we turn for the story of the genesis and
> growth of this great blessing in America. **There is an
> effort, in evidence in the secular and religious press
> of America,** and, in some sections, in many of our
> public schools, **to rob both Williams and the Bap-
> tists of their crown of glory. In certain quarters both
> Protestants and Catholics are attributing the honor
> of giving birth to religious liberty to communions
> which centuries ago persecuted our Baptist forefa-
> thers unto banishment and death.**[107]

Of William Federer and David Barton

Sitting on the shelves of a large number of Baptist
preachers is the 2000 paperback, *America's God and
Country*. The Roman Catholic author, William Federer,
compiled it. The book is a collection of quotes from
America's past and contains a wealth of information on
the religious aspect of early American rhetoric. I think
the book was designed to provide ammunition in the
current culture war. The war has made Americans pay
attention to history.

This would have been a wonderful opportunity to
go back to colonial times and beyond to retrace the
struggle for liberty. How helpful it would have been to
re-acquaint Americans with the glorious struggle of the
dissenters of Europe and England and the patient suffering of the Baptists of New England, Georgia and Virginia. For over 80 years, the American public had been
deceived about the Christian Heritage of their nation.
Now at last, the record could be set straight concerning

---

[107] Arthur B. Strickland, *Roger Williams, Prophet and Pioneer of
Soul Liberty* (Boston: The Judson Press, 1919), xiv.

John Clarke, Roger Williams, Rhode Island and Virginia.

Unfortunately, *America's God and Country* tells us nothing about Clarke, Williams, Rhode Island or Virginia. In fact the only quote in *America's God and Country* from any of the main players in American liberty is a convoluted quote attributed to Roger Williams on page 694:

> When they have opened a gap in the hedge or wall of separation between the garden of the church and the wilderness of the world, God hath ever broken down the wall itself...And that there fore if He will eer please to restore His garden and paradise again, it must of necessity be walled in peculiarly unto Himself from the world...[108]

The quote is unrecognizable. William J. Federer fails to mention Williams' most important work and foundational argument for liberty, *The Bloudy Tenet of Persecution*. The source for the convoluted quote is listed as John Eidsmoe's *Christianity and the Constitution* and David Barton's *The Myth of Separation*.

John Eidsmoe, David Barton, and other Reformed sources are cited throughout the pages of *America's God and Country*. For instance, in Federer's section devoted to George Washington there are over 70 quotes. In those quotes for Washington, David Barton's name appears 19 times. There is very little primary documentation. While Catherine Millard, Peter Marshall, David Manuel, and other catholic Reformed writers appear as sources, David Barton is the prime source.

The works of David Barton are fast becoming the new standard in American history for Christians. In fact, you could say he is enjoying an "orthodoxy." He is currently in demand as a public speaker, and is a favorite on Pat Robertson's 700 Club.

---

[108] William J. Federer, *America's God and Country* (St. Louis, MO: Amerisearch, 2000), 694.

He has not been free of criticism. In an amazing admission, Barton acknowledged 14 misquotes in his *Myth of Separation* book. You may view the misquotes on his website at http://www.wallbuilders.com/resources/. The James Madison "quote" about the 10 commandments is the most controversial. Barton admitted it could not be substantiated. Madison supposedly said:

> We have staked the whole future of American civilization, not upon the power of government, far from it. We have staked the future of all of our political institutions upon the capacity of each and all of us to govern ourselves... according to the Ten Commandments of God.

A *reconstructionist*/theocrat sure could use Madison's inaccurate quote. While James Madison said plenty of things to establish **liberty**, he never supported the establishment of a theocracy. And he never said the above quote. It is absolutely amazing how many times this misquote appears in books and on websites.

While Barton's handling of historical court cases seems accurate, his handling of American history omits the Baptist Christians of this country, and consequently, is damaging to American principles.

I am not accusing David Barton of deceit, I cannot know his heart, but his works are devoid of Baptist testimony. He freely quotes George Bancroft, the nineteenth century historian, but omits Bancroft's treatment of the Baptists. He seems to ignore I. B. Richman, John Fiske, Vernon Louis Parrington, James Ernst, Samuel Brockunier and Harvard's David Little.

The Myth of Separation is Barton's most popular book and started his career in writing. In "*Myth*," he attempts to explain the principles of American liberty as found in the first amendment of the Constitution. He avoids mentioning the influences of Roger Williams, John Clarke, Isaac Backus, or John Leland. In doing this, he omits the Baptist struggle that resulted in the rejection of ecclesiastical control of civil government. *The Myth of Seperation* examines the Baptist doctrine of church-state separation without discussing the Baptists. Does this not seem strange? Barton mentions Williams only once, as "one of the Baptists' own prominent ministers." Is it possible that Barton is ignorant of Williams and the Baptists?

On page 42 of *The Myth of Seperation,* Barton points out that Thomas Jefferson borrowed the words of Roger Williams when he used the "wall of separation" phrase to explain the intent of the First Amendment. Barton is correct. He then uses the convoluted quotation that Federer copies in *America's God and Country.*

Obviously, if David Barton is that familiar with Jefferson borrowing from Williams, he is probably familiar with Williams himself. Perhaps he just doesn't want to tell this part of history to his audience.

> How to identify a catholic Reformed history book:
> 1. No mention of the ancient evangelical parties such as the Donatists, Waldensians and Paulicians; or, they are condemned as heretics.
> 2. No mention of the suffering of the Baptists and other dissenters.
> 3. Relegation of Roger Williams to second class status. His influence through *The Bloody Tenet,* will be ignored. Backus and Leland ignored.
> 4. Elevation of John Calvin, Zwingli, Luther or John Winthrop.
> 5. Puritans given credit for founding the country.
> 6. No discussion of the dangers of theocracy and its twin doctrine of persecution.
> 7. Use of McFetridge and Boettner as historical authorities.
> 8. Criticism of Rhode Island or Virginia.
> 9. No clarification between freedom, liberty, and toleration.
> 10. No mention of Shubal Stearns, Samuel Harriss or the Separate Baptist revival.

I regretfully say, Baptist Christians should be wary of Barton. He plays a large part in falsely crediting the tyrannical catholic Reformed for the American principles of liberty. In order to be good stewards of information, we should want to know the theology that runs David Barton.

In the acknowledgments of *The Myth of Separation*, Barton gives "special honor" to Dr. John Eidsmoe, Peter Marshall and David Manuel. These three men are catholic Reformed writers. In fact, they are the foundational writers of an entire family of Christian history books. This family of history books has effectively written out the Baptists.

Liberal historians from 1920-1970, rewrote American history and deleted the Christian influence. However, that fact does not empower the catholic Reformed writers to delete the Baptists from their rightful place in history. I wonder if this is part of "the war?" If so, would not Rushdoony and company endorse such action?

The first book by the catholic Reformed to gain notoriety was the 1977 covenant way blockbuster, *The Light and the Glory* by Peter Marshall and David Manuel. Remember, Marshall and Manuel were given "special honor," by David Barton.

In the *Light and the Glory*, Manuel and Marshall revealed a strange bias against Virginia, and contempt for

Roger Williams, John Clarke and Rhode Island. Their chapter on the history of Virginia is entitled, "Damn Your Souls, Make Tobacco!" There is absolutely no reference to the Separate Baptist revival, which transformed Virginia. And there is veiled contempt for Jefferson, Madison and Washington. For those who have forgotten, those men gave us our republic, and Virginia provided four out of the first five presidents of the United States.

Of Roger Williams, Manuel and Marshall wrote:

Williams is tragic, self-righteous, **impossible, arrogant**, judgmental... to know him was to like him, no matter **how impossible** were **the tenets** he insisted upon. And **they *were* impossible**...This need to be right colored everything he did or thought; indeed, it drove him into one **untenable position** after another.[109]

According to Manuel and Marshall, Williams was arrogant and self-righteous and his **tenets** were impossible. But then, *liberty* according to the Augustinian/Calvinist *is* impossible. Manuel and Marshall bore false witness against Williams on page 193:

> "Hopefully, the Baptists of America will continue to listen to and read the writings of Augustinians."
>
> –Ray Sutton

...facing up to one's self-righteousness and repenting of it on a continuing basis—was **more than he could bring himself to accept**.[110]

On the same page, Manuel and Marshall define the *liberty of conscious*:

Liberty of conscious means..."**Nobody is going to tell me what I should do or believe**." Taken out of balance and pursued to its **extremes**..., **it becomes a license to disregard all authority** with which we do not happen to agree at the time.[111]

These are untruths. The liberty to worship God according to the dictates of ones conscious is **extreme**?! This is classic Augustinianism.

---

[109] Peter Marshall and David Manuel, *The Light and the Glory* (Tarrytown: Fleming H. Revell, 1977), 193.

[110] Ibid.

[111] Ibid.

Barton gives these men "special honor?" This may explain Barton's complete shut out of the Baptists in his materials in *Wallbuilders*.

The *Light and the Glory*, is a member of a family of Reformed history books which either bear false witness against the Baptists, or omit their sufferings and contributions. The following books comprise the catholic Reformed re-write family:

Foundational
> *Calvinism in History*, 1882, N. S. McFetridge
> *The Reformed Doctine of Predestination*, 1932, Loraine Boettner

Institutional
> *The Light and the Glory*, 1977, Peter Marshall and David Manuel
> *The Separation Illusion*, 1977, John Whitehead
> *Christianity and the Constitution*, 1987, John Eidsmoe
> *Faith and Freedom*, 1988, Benjamin Hart
> *The Myth of Separation*, 1992, David Barton
> *America's God and Country*, 2000, William J. Federer

In the above books, no mention of the suffering of the ancient Baptists is made. Martin Luther, John Calvin, and John Winthrop are proclaimed the founding fathers of the American Republic. No distinction between freedom, liberty and toleration is made. Roger Williams, John Clarke and Rhode Island are either put in a bad light, or passed over. The Puritans founded the country. There is elevation of Samuel Rutherford and downplaying of Jefferson, Madison and Washington. Virginia's role in liberty is either downplayed or denied.

Some of these books even contain the fairy tale of the Presbyterian *Mecklenburg Declaration of Independence*. This Presbyterian document was supposedly given to the Continental Congress in 1775.

(Jefferson denied its authenticity. Thirty years later the Presbyterians accused him of plagiarism.)

The family of Reformed history books is enjoying an unopposed run. As Ray Sutton said, **"Hopefully, the Baptists of America will continue to listen to and read the writings of Augustinians."**[112]

Well, this is one Baptist that hopes—**not**!

---

[112] Ray Sutton, "The Baptist Failure," *The Failure of the American Baptist Culture* (Tyler, TX: Geneva Divinity School, *Christianity and Civilization, Vol. 1*, 1982), 184.

Epilogue
Chapter 13
Theocracy, Antichrist and the
Coming Destruction of the Baptist People

James Madison and the Framers put forth a new national covenant based on William's model in 1787, and the voters' representatives ratified it in 1788. We live under its jurisdiction still. We will not live under it forever.—Gary North[113]

Baptist history, theology and sociology spell failure. The system at root centers around man. For that reason the American Baptist paradigm will go the way of man—death.
—Ray Sutton[114]

Politically, the only legitimate long-term biblical goal is the creation of a worldwide theocratic republic.
—Gary North[115]

The long-term goal of Christians in politics should be to **gain exclusive control** over the franchise. Those who refuse to submit publicly to the eternal sanctions of God by submitting to **His Church's public marks of the covenant— baptism and holy communion**—must be **denied citizenship**, just as they were in ancient Israel.—Gary North

And there came one of the seven angels which had the seven vials, and talked with me, saying unto me, Come hither; I will shew unto thee the judgment of the great whore that sitteth upon many waters: With whom the kings of the earth have

---

[113] *Political Polytheism* (Tyler, TX: Institute for Christian Economics, 1989), 371.

[114] Ray Sutton, "The Baptist Failure," *The Failure of the American Baptist Culture* (Tyler, TX: Geneva Divinity School, *Christianity and Civilization, Vol. 1*, 1982), 184.

[115] Gary North, *Political Polytheism: The Myth of Pluralism* (Tyler, TX: Institute for Christian Economics, 1989), 650.

committed fornication, and the inhabitants of the earth have been made drunk with the wine of her fornication. So he carried me away in the spirit into the wilderness: and I saw a woman sit upon a scarlet coloured beast, full of names of blasphemy, having seven heads and ten horns. And the woman was arrayed in purple and scarlet colour, and decked with gold and precious stones and pearls, having a golden cup in her hand full of abominations and filthiness of her fornication: And upon her forehead was a name written, MYSTERY, BABYLON THE GREAT, THE MOTHER OF HARLOTS AND ABOMINATIONS OF THE EARTH. And I saw the woman drunken with the blood of the saints, and with the blood of the martyrs of Jesus: and when I saw her, I wondered with great admiration. Revelation 17:1-6

The Reformed are right about one thing, we are presently engaged in a war over principles. And theology is running the engine of the war.

If you think catholic Reformed theology is harmless to the Baptists, I believe you have been subject to deception.

If you are Baptist and you think catholic Reformed theology is attractive, I believe you have been subject to deception.

Gary DeMar, home school author, Christian *Reconstructionist*, and frequent speaker at the Witherspoon School of Law wrote the book, *The Reduction of Christianity*. The foreword, written by Gary North states:

Dominion Theology teaches that we can, do and will have a kingdom of God on earth without Jesus' physical presence in Jerusalem.[116]

These people are not with the United Nations, they are not liberal theologians. They want religious dominion. Some of them, in their *New World Order*, advocate a "consistent" application of "God's Law" so that adulterers, rebellious children—and heretics, (Baptists)

---

[116] Gary DeMar and Peter J. Leithart, *The Reduction of Christianity* (Atlanta, GA: American Vision Press, 1988), xii.

are to be exterminated. We are not talking about Moslem extremists here, we are talking about a very vocal and influential faction of Calvinistic postmillennialists.

The books of the catholic Reformed re-write family are successfully reconstructing not only Baptist Christians, but the general public as well.

Catholic and Reformed theology ties the one world government to the one world religion. For this to fully develop, Christianity must become fully political. Let us look at the latest in this advancing development.

The newest book in the Reformed family is *One Nation Under Man?* by Brannon Howse, released in 2005. Howse quotes David Barton dozens of times, uses the same old and oversimplified tactic of pitting "humanism" against Christianity. A quick look at Howse's dedication page reveals his theology:

> To my children...I love you and want to preserve America's Christian history and freedoms, which are gifts from God, so you and your children's children and beyond can freely live out the Christian worldview and **create a Christian dynasty** that will impact America and the world for eternity.[117]

Brannon Howse holds his *Christian Worldview Weekends* in churches, resorts and *Baptist* churches across the country.

Howse uses David Barton, John Whitehead, John Eidsmoe, Gary DeMar and D. James Kennedy to back up his ideas. They are all catholic Reformed history re-writers. And who published Howse's book? Southern *Baptist* Broadman and Holman Publishers!

My belief is that the problems in America are not caused by humanism, but by *paganism*. Paganism, which includes humanistic and evolutionary ideas, can only be checked by the strength of God's churches. Paganism is kept in check by preaching.

---

[117] Brannon Howse, *One Nation Under Man?* (Nashville: Broadman and Holman Pub., 2005), dedication page.

Compromised preaching grieves the Holy Ghost making revival and awakening impossible. How we have missed the mark on this important issue!

Ignoring this issue, Brannon Howse gives an assist to the *New World Order* by insisting "True Conservatism" *is* "Christianity." On page 65 of *One Nation Under Man?* Howse writes:

> The foundation, then, on which a conservative bases his or her positions on important issues is the Christian worldview. Most conservatives, **knowingly or unknowingly**, have been influenced by the same biblical worldview on which the Founders based their structure for America's legal, governmental, economic, and ethical system.[118]

Am I believing my eyes? TO BE A CONSERVATIVE MEANS YOU ARE A CHRISTIAN? Chapter eight in Howse's book is entitled *Why Humanism (Modern-day Liberalism) Is a Lie and Christianity (True Conservatism) Is the Truth.* Is he really saying, "if you are liberal (I assume politically) you are *not* a Christian," and "if you are a Conservative you *are* a Christian?"

When they are candid, the Reformed have a problem with "experimental religion," or what evangelicals acknowledge as "ye must be born again." This issue was at the heart of the banishment of Dr. John Clarke and the opinionists from Boston in 1637.[119] If you are predestined to eternal life *before* birth, then the "new birth" is not necessary. A conservative is a Christian, born again or not. We are heading for one whopper of a union of *conservative* Christianity.

In the past few years, Andrew Sandlin, John Whitehead, Gary DeMar and many others have tried to "officially" distance themselves from Reformed *Reconstructionism.* However, we must understand, it is not *Reconstructionism* alone, it is Catholic and Reformed

---

[118] Ibid., 65.

[119] See *America in Crimson Red* (Arnold, MO: Prairie Fire Press, 2004), 24-37.

THEOLOGY, with its emphasis on infant baptism, sacraments, theocracy and postmillennialism that is damaging to the Republic.

There is coming a day when the current group of churches which call themselves "Baptist" will cease to be Baptist. In some cases this has already happened. If your reaction to that is no reaction then it probably has already happened to you. In my opinion, you have already been reconstructed.

If we do not reconnect with our Baptist heritage and theology, our churches will either embrace religious liberalism or be assimilated into the Reformed movement.

If this seems improbable, allow me to share with you a notable current event. You will remember from chapter five of our briefing, the International Baptist Network unified under the five fundamentals of the 1910 Synod of the Northern Presbyterian Church. Tragically, **affirmation of believer's baptism**, the issue upon which thousands of our forefathers were martyred, seems to have become irrelevant. A most vivid illustration of this current trend is found in the ministry of the immensely popular John Piper.

Piper is the author of the best seller, *Desiring God*. His church, Bethlehem Baptist in Minneapolis, Minnesota is a leading church in the Reformed Baptist movement.

In September of 2005, Piper and the elders of Bethlehem Baptist Church proposed a change in the constitution of their church. To their congregation, Piper and the board wrote:

> The most obvious change... is allowing the **possibility that a person may become a member who has not been baptized by immersion** as a believer but who regards the baptismal ritual he received in **in-**

fancy not as regenerating, but nevertheless (as with most Presbyterians) in such a way that it would violate his conscience to be baptized as a believer. The elders are proposing that **under certain conditions such persons be admitted to full membership**.

After more than three years of study and prayer and discussion of this issue, the Council of Elders believes that membership requirements at Bethlehem **should move toward being roughly the same as the requirements for membership in the universal body of Christ**.[120]

John Piper and his elders believe that the tenets of catholic Reformed Calvinism are much more important than the distinctive Baptist Christian tenet of believer's baptism. They wrote:

It is troubling that we require agreement on the doctrine of baptism but not on **more important matters** like the nature of God's **sovereign grace**, the way of salvation by **effectual calling**, the **gift of faith**, the nature and power of **depravity**, the freedom of the will, the work of God in the **perseverance** of the saints, etc.[121]

After reading the above points of Calvinism to his congregation, Piper said, **"All of those things are more important than** agreeing on the time and mode of **baptism** in my judgment. **All of them**...the great **reformed truths** that we love."[122]

So on we go. The antichrist theocracy demands the demise of Baptist principles, reduction of believer's baptism in favor of infant sprinkling, and disregard for the dispensation or new covenant of the church age.

---

[120] John Piper, "What the Elders Are Proposing: Amendments to the Constitution and By-Laws" August 31, 2005. http://www.desiringgod.org/library/fresh_words/2005/083105.html

[121] John Piper, Alex Chediak and Tom Steller, "Baptism and Church Membership At Bethlehem Baptist Church, Eight Recommendations for Constitutional Revision," August 9, 2005. p. 19. http://www.desiringgod.org/library

[122] Ibid., September 14, 2005.

The "universal" church as theocratic Israel by definition is a worldwide religion. The Reformed play into the hands of antichrist by promoting "universal church" and theocratic ideas.

The Reformed promote political activism. They believe the government of the United States needs to be changed to include an ecclesiastical establishment. Their theology demands it. They are playing into the hands of the antichrist theocracy, which will one day grip the earth.

Theocracies do not work. Only one theocracy was ordained in history, that being the theocracy of Israel. The gentile theocracy was attempted for nearly 1000 years. It didn't work.

However, antichrist will set up *his* theocracy shortly. It is known presently as the **New World Order**. Don't be deceived, it is nothing but the **Old World Order**. All Baptist sentiment will die with its appearance. Then something the postmillennial Catholics and Reformers deny will happen—**seven** years after the inception of the *New World Order*, Jesus Christ will abruptly return, throw the antichrist out of Jerusalem and into Hell, and set up **His own** theocracy.

Epilogue
Chapter 14
Repairing America through Her Principles of Liberty

> Religion, as well as reason, confirms the soundness of those principles on which our government has been founded and its rights asserted.
> —Thomas Jefferson

> The constitutional freedom of religion [is] the most inalienable and sacred of all human rights.
> —Thomas Jefferson

> Religious liberty has unchained the Bible, scattered the darkness of superstition, flooded our continent with light and blessing. It has toppled selfish autocrats from their thrones, it has unlocked the shackles from the feet of millions who were living in spiritual and physical slavery. Religious liberty opens the doors and lets God's sunlight of truth enter to warm and bless the world.
> —Arthur B. Strickland[123]

The Christians of the 70's and 80's panicked. A culture war really did begin.

No doubt our society is still in danger. We continue to have big problems with the ACLU and a runaway judiciary. And crime, adultery, theft, abortion, homosexuality and selfishness run rampant. We need change. We need revival. But we must not revise history to prove our points. We cannot fix America by changing her form of government. Believe me, the catholic Reformed, when they are candid, advocate a change in our *form* of government. Severing us from our foundation is the first step to changing the form.

What should we do? I propose four objectives:

---

[123] Arthur B. Strickland *Roger Williams, Prophet and Pioneer of Soul Liberty* (Boston: The Judson Press, 1919), xiv.

- Baptist Christians need to answer their theological enemies and reconnect with their heritage.
- Baptist Christian schools need proper Bible, history, and civics curriculum.
- The American public needs to reconnect with the principles of the Declaration of Independence and the fundamental basis of American law. In order to do this we must examine the writings of Isaac Backus and John Leland.
- Finally, a working knowledge of the amendment process must become common.

Those on the Christian Right, tainted with *Reconstructionism* and ideas of theocracy, have positioned themselves as spokesmen for Christians in America. They believe something is wrong with America. However, in their zeal to fix America some have been less than honest.

We are not going to get anywhere lying about our history. We have lost our credibility by re-writing American history. Our forefathers rejected theocracy and we must concur. An honest assessment of "original intent" is in order.

Is this a Christian nation? Yes, but only if Christians are in it. Is America a theocracy with judgements based on Biblical law and established interpretations? No, even Jesus taught that the theocracy of Israel was fulfilled with His death burial and resurrection. No, America is a nation with *liberty*. We Christians make laws only if we influence and/or occupy Congress and our principles prevail.

The theocrats such as John Eidsmoe, Peter Marshall, and David Barton do not seem to understand. The nation became a battleground of free exercise. And while their Reformed ancestors were complaining about the "antichristian" and "covenant breaking" Constitution, God sent wave after wave of revival. James Madison understood this. Madison led the protest against forced tithes (called assessments) in Virginia.

He argued that establishing a denomination or religion would cripple the efforts of all denominations to preach the Gospel to the lost. Madison wrote:

> The first wish of those who enjoy this precious gift [of salvation] ought to be that it may be imparted to the whole race of mankind. [The Bill of Assessments] at once **discourages those** who are strangers to the light of revelation **from coming into the Region of it**; and countenances by example the nations who continue in darkness, in shutting out those who might convey it to them.[124]

In other words, James Madison predicted that religious liberty would make America a haven for the lost. Free Christianity, with no establishment, would be empowered to win the lost to this "precious gift." In reality, Madison was predicting future revival and missions. He was right on target.

You see, it is not so important what the founders and framers said "about God," we all know the vast majority of them believed "in God." It is most important what they said about religion and civil government. That is what needs to be examined.

Madison became the father or "architect" of the Constitution. His friendship with the Baptists of Virginia garnered their support for the Constitution as he promised and delivered the Bill of Rights. What is never mentioned in the catholic Reformed history books is that a good number of Presbyterians were not happy with the Constitution. In 1812, Timothy Dwight, President of Yale College announced to the Yale chapel:

> The nation has offended Providence. We formed our Constitution without any acknowledgement of God...we commenced our national existence under the present system, without God.[125]

---

[124] James Madison, *Memorial and Remonstrance*.

[125] Isaac Kramnick and R. Laurence Moore, *The Godless Constitution: The case against Religious Correctness* (New York: Norton, 1996), 105-6.

Other groups such as the Reformed Presbyterian Church of North America (Covenanters) have never embraced the Constitution as the form of our government.

While the Reformed Protestants were complaining about the new Constitution, the Baptists and the Methodists rode off to save the country from a burning Hell. The Presbyterians eventually tried to join in the *War for Souls*, but were derailed by the processes at Princeton which could not train enough preachers to keep pace with the converts. The Baptists fought with the predestinarians in their own ranks who could not believe a "sovereign" God could save so many people so fast. The debates over the tenets of Calvin were actually good stimulation in the *War for Souls*.

So great was the Baptist revival through Kentucky that new churches were springing up *daily*. Ah, that was America.

I am saying, the country was just fine with the form of government it had.

Today, admittedly, there are problems. But we do not have to destroy the form and instigate theocracy to fix it. The country, founded on Baptist principles, guaranteed religious liberty to all citizens by the adoption of the first amendment. Do we disregard the first amendment, or claim that the establishment clause is a *myth* or an *illusion*? What will that accomplish? The church and the state being separate in their jurisdiction is not a *myth*, it is a safeguard against hundreds of years of *religious* tyranny.

What does the first amendment say exactly?

Congress shall make **no law** respecting an **establishment** of religion, or **prohibiting the free exercise thereof**; or abridging the freedom of speech, or of the press; or the right of the people peaceably to assemble, and to petition the Government for a redress of grievances.

We cannot do away with the establishment clause of the first amendment (erroneously called separation of church and state), nor should we amend the abolishment of religious tests, as set forth in Article 6 clause 3. Neither should we stop the application of the Fourteenth Amendment as some in the Religious Right have suggested. As I recall, we fought a civil war over that one.

The founders knew exactly that the first amendment was adopted for the dissenters and Baptists in this country. Congress can make no law to establish, and no law to prohibit free exercise of religion.

However, one flaw in a nearly flawless constitutional frame was the failure of the framers to envision a day when a citizen of the United States would force others to deny the existence of God. Think of it. Not Jefferson, not Madison, not Witherspoon, not even ol' Tom Paine could have imagined the evil of a Madalyn Murray O' Hair.

The O' Hair's of the world forced the federal judiciary to rule on issues unimaginable to the framers. It was not a part of their *original mindset.*

Original mindset is what we should be after here. *The original mindset* of the framers was **local government**. The Civil War destroyed some of that *original mindset*, but there is no reason why we couldn't get some of it back.

What part of the frame needs to be fixed? The founders and framers could have **never envisioned the current course of the courts**. That the federal judiciary is out of control is acknowledged by all. But what are we to do about it?

Let's don't panic. Religious leaders such as Gary Bauer have said that Christians just want a place at the table. We have that place. Let us use it the right way. The liberal left is aware of the *Reconstructionist* leanings of the right. And they are angry about it. And honestly I do not blame them. No one in their right mind wants to have a theocracy that enforces the conscience (the first table of the law). Any proposal, until antichrist, that hints at religious establishment is going to lose.

We must operate within the form given to us. And that would mean a Constitutional amendment.

June 17, 1963 was the day America should have begun working on the defect of the frame of the Constitution. That was the day the Supreme Court ruled prayer in the public schools was "un-Constitutional."

That ruling was followed by Abington v. Schempp which threw Bible reading out of our schools. Then the 1980 Stone v. Graham case removed the Ten Commandments from the classroom.

In 1963, a stream of protest followed the first case. There were 146 resolutions, designed to amend the Constitution to override the findings of the American Supremes. One such amendment proposal read, "Nothing in this Constitution shall be deemed to prohibit the offering, reading from, or listening to prayers of biblical scriptures, if participation therein is on a voluntary basis, in any governmental or public school, institution, or place."[126]

The proposal was deemed too controversial. My opinion is that it was too narrow and too close to establishment.

To fix the flaw an amendment to the Constitution must weld us back to the frame.

Most Americans are familiar with the case of Roy Moore, former Chief Justice of the Alabama Supreme Court. Moore had placed a monument in honor of the Ten Commandments in the Supreme Court building in Birmingham. As official custodian of the building, he deemed it appropriate. A federal court ruled he must remove the monument, citing the establishment clause from the first amendment. When Moore refused, he was removed from office.

Judge Moore has since formed the *Foundation of Moral Law*, headquartered in Montgomery, Alabama. He is lecturing here and there around the country, and has recently announced his candidacy in the 2006 race

---

[126] John Whitehead, *The Separation Illusion* (Milford, MI: Mott Media, Inc., 1977), 119.

for governor of Alabama. His tie to Reformed *Reconstructionism* is his involvement in the Witherspoon School of Law.

In 2005 the Witherspoon School featured Howard Phillips, Douglas W. Phillips, Justice Tom Parker, Dr. Edwin Vieira, Dr. Paul Jehle, John Eidsmoe, and William Einwechter, vice president of the National Reform Association. It was Einwechter who said, "to make the Declaration of Independence into a fundamental statement of the political philosophy upon which the United States was founded is both misguided and futile."[127]

Is Roy Moore a *Reconstructionist*? He is a Southern Baptist, but his circle certainly is postmillennial, Reformed and *Reconstructionist*.

Moore's organization, through Senator Shelby, has proposed Bill S. 520 to amend the U. S. Constitution. Their proposal is named the Constitution Restoration Act. It was presented to the Senate of the United States on March 3, 2005. Part of it read:

> Sec. 1260. Matters not reviewable.
>
> Notwithstanding any other provision of this chapter, the Supreme Court shall not have jurisdiction to review, by appeal, writ of certiorari, or otherwise, any matter to the extent that relief is sought against an entity of Federal, State, or local government, or against an officer or agent of Federal, State, or local government (whether or not acting in official or personal capacity), concerning that entity's, officer's, or agent's acknowledgment of God as the sovereign source of law, liberty, or government.

It is an ambitious attempt. However, it may be that the bill for the amendment is too narrow, and to some, may come across as a publicity stunt. I do not believe that was the intention. This issue is very pivotal for our times; it is about the civil rights of citizens and public

---

[127] William Einwechter, "Declaration of Independence and National Renewal" (Pittsburgh, PA: *The Christian Statesman*, July-Aug. 2000)

servants who want to express their religious convictions.

American Christians need to ask, "If Judge Moore was Muslim, would he have been able, as custodian of the court building, to place a monument to the Koran?" The only consistent answer according to the principles of our republic is that **the people** of Alabama should decide.

Think about the first amendment which says, ***Congress*** shall make **no law** respecting an **establishment** of religion, or **prohibiting the free exercise thereof**; or abridging the freedom of speech, or of the press; or the right of the people peaceably to assemble, and to petition the Government for a redress of grievances.

The first amendment plainly states that the federal Congress cannot legislate **for or against** religious exercise. It should follow that if the federal *Congress* cannot legislate religious exercise, then neither should the federal *Courts* exercise judgement over religious exercise. This definitely was implied. So much was it understood that no federal court wrestled with denying religious exercise for 75 years.

I believe that an amendment that would best serve the entire nation is one that would voice the implied restriction. Let's face it, religious exercise is not the business of the federal government. **All federal courts should throw every case involving religious exercise back to their local concerns**.

Perhaps a better bill for an amendment might read:

All judiciary matters pertaining **to the free exercise of religion** by either private citizens or public officials shall be limited to the states.

Or:

The federal judiciary shall have no jurisdiction in cases concerning the **establishment** of religion, or **prohibiting the free exercise thereof**; or abridging the freedom of speech, or of the press; or the right of the people peaceably to assemble, and to petition the Government for a redress of grievances.

Such an amendment would curtail the temptation towards theocracy and stimulate the Christian public to more rousing debate. It would also motivate Christians to sway public opinion by the best scriptural means— **winning the lost to Christ, birthing churches and praying for revival**.

INDEX

INDEX

INDEX

Paschal, G. W.: 24f, 39, 39f
Paulicians: 12, 35, 91, 97
Pauline Worldview: 6, 7
Pedobaptist historians: 2, 3
Petrobrussians: 2, 12
Phillips, Doug: 96
Piper, John: 111-112
Postmillennial(ism): 14, 30, 33, 47, 48, 109, 111, 113, 120
Predestination: 30, 105
Presbyterian Church, General Assembly of the Northern: 43
Presbyterian(s): 2, 3, 15, 17, 19, 20, 31-34, 37, 43, 45, 63, 70, 71, 81-84, 86-89, 95, 105, 111, 112, 116, 117
Puritans: 7, 17, 56, 76, 92, 94, 105
Quakers: 17, 56, 66, 93
Reconstructionist(s): 30, 33-35, 54, 73, 75, 81, 83-88,91-93,108, 118, 120
Reformed Doctine of Predestination: 105
Richman, I. B.: 63, 101
Rogers, Jay: 96
Roman Catholic: 2, 3, 13, 41, 91
Roman Catholic historian: 3
Rushdoony, R. J.: 9, 31, 32, 34, 46, 73, 75, 79, 82, 83, 86, 87, 96, 97, 103
Rutherford, Samuel: 34, 68,69, 73, 74, 81, 82, 87, 94, 105
Sandlin, Andrew: 32
Scammon, Rachel Thurber: 41
Schaeffer, Francis: 80, 81, 86, 87
Schaff, Phillip: 15f
Separate Baptists: 17, 39-41, 88, 89, 93-95, 103
Separation Illusion: 105
Shurden, Walter: 24, 28
Smith, John B.: 20
Southern Baptist Seminary: 21
Southern Baptist Convention: 23, 44
Spencer, J. H.: 22
Spittlehouse, John: 2, 26
Spurgeon, Charles: 1, 2, 3, 7, 26, 28, 37
Stearns, Shubal: 37, 39-41, 85, 88, 93-95
Stennett, Samuel: 40
Straus, Oscar: 67
Strickland, Arthur B.: 13f, 38f, 63f, 67f, 99f, 104f,114
Sutton, Ray: 76, 77, 104, 106, 107
Talmage, T. DeWitt: 37
Taylor, John: 41

ABOUT THE AUTHOR

James R. Beller is a native of St. Louis, Missouri. He grew up on the "South Side" and attended St. Pius V. grade school on Utah and Grand Avenue.

In his high school days the author was born again after reading Gospel tracts that had been given to his mother. Four years later, while attending a local state university, he surrendered to the Gospel ministry and enrolled in Bible college. While in college, he met his wife, Vickie.

James has pastored the Arnold Baptist Tabernacle in Jefferson County, Missouri since 1987. The church has enjoyed good growth from a storefront to its present properties, which include a lovely auditorium completed in 1994.

The church has planted five other churches in the St. Louis and Missouri areas since 1996—The Solid Rock Baptist Church in Rock Hill, Missouri; the South Broadway Baptist Chapel, St. Louis, Missouri: the Victory Independent Baptist Church in St. Louis; Blessed Hope Baptist Church in Farmington, Missouri; and Grace Independent Baptist Church in High Ridge, Missouri. Arnold Baptist Tabernacle is currently assisting in planting a sixth independent Baptist church in the St. Louis, Missouri area.

Pastor Beller is the author of numerous booklets on doctrine and church planting. He is the author of the popular historical narratives, *The Soul of St. Louis*, and *America in Crimson Red*, and the widely used *Collegiate Baptist History Workbook*. He and his wife have four children: Jeremy, Nicole, Zackary and Katherine.

Visit

baptistchristianworldview.com

Read the latest articles on the current war over first principles.

From Prairie Fire Press  PRAIRIE FIRE PRESS

DVDs

Shubal Stearns and the Greatest American Revival (60 min.)
~fall 2006
Follow the life of America's great pioneer preacher. Interviews and insight on how God used the Separate Baptists.

A True History of American Liberty (60 min.)
~spring 2006
Join us as we take you into the pit of Newgate prison, to the Isle of Rhodes, and to Philadelphia. A must see for every citizen or new citizen.

Fundamentals of American Civics and Government (40 min.)
~fall 2006
What is the form and frame of American government? What is the scriptural basis for it? How are we to use this frame as good citizens?

BOOKS

America in Crimson Red (607 pages) hardback
Narrative on the history of the Baptists in America 1620-1905.

The Coming Destruction of the Baptist People (120 pages)
Explains why Baptist people have no connection to their own heritage.

The Collegiate Baptist History Workbook (250 pages)
Text used in a large number of Colleges. Church history from A.D. 31 to the twenty-first century.

The Theocracy Conspiracy (120 pages) by John Hardin
Fascinating look at conspiracy, predestination and salvation.

Stearns-Marshall Publications

Texts and Curriculum for the Baptist Christian School and Home School

HISTORY

A Baptist History Primer A-Z by Nathan Deatrick
~fall 2006
Wonderful learning tool for k-1st grade. 26 poems and illustrations follow the alphabet and introduce Baptist Christian testimony and principles.

America from Sea to Shining Sea
~fall 2006
American history and Social Studies primer for 1st grade.

God's People in the Wide, Wide, World
~fall 2006
World history primer for Baptist school kids. 2nd grade.

American Government in Baptist Christian Perspective 11/12th gr.
~fall 2006
Puts into working knowledge the form and frame of America's government.

Survey of Baptist Truth and Testimony 11/12th grade.
~summer 2006
The Baptist Workbook for High School. Covers from A.D. 31 to the twenty-first century.

BIBLE

Bible in Many Colors 1ST grade.
~fall 2006
Reader and Bible primer for first grade.

High School Bible by Jerry Ross 11/12 grade.
~fall 2006
High School Bible class written by one of America's most effective pastors to young people.

visit **baptistchristianworldview.com** for pricing and availability or call 314-606-7326